TITANIC
YOUNG SURVIVORS

By Allan Zullo

SCHOLASTIC INC.

To my grandson Jack Manausa, whose spirited
nature, charming personality, and cheerful attitude
are unsinkable.
—A.Z.

ISBN 978-0-545-81839-1

12 11 10 9 8 7 6 5 4 3   15 16 17 18 19 20 21/0

Printed in the U.S.A.   40
This edition first printing, January 2016

Acknowledgments

I am extremely grateful for the cooperation I received from the research staff at the Titanic Museum Attractions in Branson, Missouri, and Pigeon Forge, Tennessee (titanicattraction.com), and to Ed and Karen Kamuda, of the Titanic Historical Society.

In addition, I wish to thank the relatives of survivors who wrote accounts of their experiences, which helped immensely in my research. Special thanks go to David Haisman and Phyllis Ryerse.

Author's Note

The RMS *Titanic* carried 2,208 passengers and crewmembers. Among them were 195 unmarried young people between 10 weeks old and 17 years old. Sadly, less than half of them—only 86—survived.

There's a fascinating story behind each kid on that ill-fated ship. I wish I could write something about every one of them, but, of course, that's not possible. Instead, I have written ten stories that reflect what happened on that terrible night of April 14–15, 1912, as seen through the eyes of children. All had their own unique experience, depending on the class (first, second, or third) and the lifeboat they were in.

Two teenage survivors never even made it into a lifeboat. Jack Thayer, the youngest person to leap into the frigid water and live, clung to an overturned sinking lifeboat throughout the cold night. So did John Collins, the youngest crewmember to survive, after he

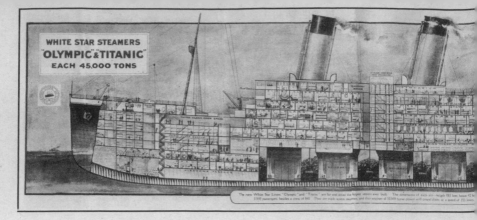

was swept off the *Titanic* while trying to save an infant.

Kids like 12-year-old Ruth Becker showed remarkable courage in the ship's final minutes. When she saw her mother and little brother leave in a lifeboat without her, Ruth refused to panic and managed to save herself. Many young people boarding lifeboats faced heartbreak, waving good-bye to their fathers, who remained on the sinking ship. Eleven-year-old Billy Carter wept when he was forced to leave his beloved dog behind before the boy was allowed into a lifeboat.

Some young survivors had rather bizarre experiences on board. Fifteen-year-old Edith Brown heard ominous premonitions from passengers and family that the ship was doomed. And nine-year-old Willie Coutts wore a straw hat that nearly cost him his life.

Because this tragedy happened back in 1912, no survivor is still alive to talk about it. (The last remaining survivor, Millvina Dean, who was only ten weeks old at the time the ship sank, died in England in 2009 at the age of 97.) So for this book, I read hundreds of

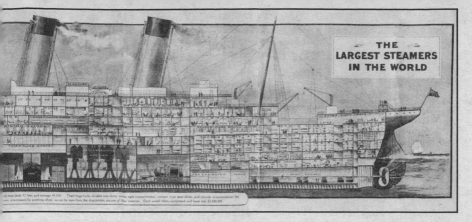

THE LARGEST STEAMERS IN THE WORLD

newspaper and magazine accounts, the official transcripts of U.S. Senate and British commission hearings on the sinking of the *Titanic,* oral histories and memoirs from survivors, and books about the disaster, as well as watched videos of survivor interviews. In addition, I relied on information supplied by relatives of survivors; the Titanic Historical Society; the Titanic Museums in Branson, Missouri, and Pigeon Forge, Tennessee; and websites devoted to the *Titanic,* especially encyclopedia-titanica.org, titanic-titanic.com, titanic1 .org, titanicinquiry.org, and rmstitanic.net.

From all this source material, I have tried to piece together an accurate accounting of the experiences of young survivors. The dialogue, which has been recreated, is based on their own recollections. But there is margin for error. At hearings in New York and London, passengers and crewmembers sometimes gave conflicting testimony. Even basic facts such as the number of people aboard the *Titanic* and the number of those saved have been in dispute to this very day.

It wasn't unusual for a survivor to give slightly different versions of his or her account of what happened. Memories over time occasionally grew fuzzy. In some cases, mistaken beliefs were repeated so often they turned into myths that have survived for decades. Part of the blame lay with the sensational newspaper coverage back then. Reporters were notorious for exaggerating the truth—and for making up facts solely for dramatic effect.

In an effort to make this book as accurate as possible, I enlisted the help of the research staff at the Titanic Museums. The researchers read over the manuscript, looking for myths, misconceptions, and mistakes. I made changes based on their recommendations.

To help you with the many nautical terms used in the book, I have included a glossary in the back.

No one will ever know exactly what went through the minds of these young people as the *Titanic* was sinking. Undoubtedly, the calamity impacted the rest of their lives in big ways and small. Some suffered from nightmares or emotionally painful reminders at random times while others put the experience behind them and moved on with their lives. Some chose not to talk about the *Titanic* while others relished the opportunity to tell their story to anyone who would listen.

Although the young survivors are no longer with us, their stories of heartache and triumph, bravery and sacrifice live on.

—A.Z.

Contents

The Sinking of the *Titanic*

No maritime disaster in modern history has captivated the public's imagination more than the sinking of the RMS *Titanic*. Over the years, countless books and articles have examined every conceivable angle of the calamity. Movies have re-created gripping scenes from that fateful night. Museums have been built dedicated solely to the ship and the people she was transporting. Websites, message boards, forums, and discussion groups have analyzed and debated all aspects of the passengers, crew, and ship.

There have been worse peacetime tragedies at sea before and after the *Titanic*'s doomed journey. (The Chinese junk *Tek Sing* struck a reef and sank in 1822, killing at least 1,600 persons; the Philippine ferry *Doña Paz* went down in 1987, claiming more than 4,300 lives.) But in terms of sheer worldwide interest, nothing compares with the *Titanic*—history's most famous (and arguably most infamous) ship.

On April 10, 1912, the majestic steamship set off on her maiden voyage from Southampton, England, bound for New York City with 2,208 passengers and crewmembers on board. She stopped in Cherbourg, France, and Queenstown, Ireland, before heading out into the Atlantic. Four days into the crossing, at 11:40 P.M., the ship struck an iceberg. Less than three hours later—at 2:20 A.M., April 15—she sank, taking the lives of an estimated 1,502 passengers and crewmembers. Reportedly, only 712 people were saved—including 86 children.

On so many levels, the disaster stunned people around the globe.

The sinking was simply unimaginable. During the construction of the *Titanic* and her sister ship the *Olympic*, her British owner, the White Star Line, published a 1910 publicity brochure boasting "as far as it is possible to do so, these two wonderful vessels are designed to be unsinkable." A major industry publication called her "practically unsinkable." But by the time the *Titanic* was ready to sail, the general public had ignored the word "practically" and believed she truly *was* "unsinkable."

The *Titanic* was the technological marvel of her time—the largest moving man-made object in the world. She was 882 feet 9 inches long (the length of almost three football fields) and 92 feet wide (slightly more than the major league distance from home plate to first base). From the waterline to the top deck, she rose 60.5 feet. She had ten decks—the Boat Deck (the top one), then Decks A through G and two more at the bottom for the equipment and cargo. The four-funneled steamship was equipped with 29 boilers fired by 159 coal-burning furnaces to create the steam that powered her three massive propellers. Built to carry more than 3,500 passengers and crew, she could reach a speed of 23 knots (26 miles an hour) and make the Atlantic crossing in a week—an amazing feat back then. She had a double hull and 16 watertight compartments that were designed to keep her afloat in case some of them were breeched.

While most people lit their homes with gas lanterns, *Titanic* had electric lights in all the cabins and electric heaters in all the first-class staterooms. Her wireless radio was capable of transmitting messages up to 1,200 miles away, depending on the weather. She had a 50-telephone switchboard, a state-of-the-art hospital, and four elevators for the use of first- and second-class passengers.

When it came to luxury, the *Titanic* couldn't be matched. Her public rooms were adorned with ornate wood-carved paneling, elaborate glass domes, works of art, and the finest furnishings. She featured a heated swimming pool, a fully-equipped gymnasium, a regulation squash court, a Turkish bath (a fancy sauna), a darkroom for amateur photographers, gourmet restaurants, barbershops, libraries, and lounges. The accommodations were as good, if not better, than most hotels of that era.

She was an awesome wonder at a time when Americans were toiling incredibly hard just to make ends meet. In 1912, the annual salary for the average worker was $850. Many children worked in cotton mills, factories, and coal mines for pennies a day. Horse and buggies shared rutted and muddy roads with automobiles, like the Model T Ford, which was becoming affordable for the working class. To travel long distances, people took a train or boat. Airplanes were flown mostly at air shows and for the military. Five months before the *Titanic*'s maiden voyage, the first plane flew from coast to coast—in 84 days. Few people had telephones, so they communicated by writing letters or going down to the local telegraph office. For entertainment, they went to the picture show to watch silent movies or to the theater to see live variety shows called vaudeville. Back then, the *Titanic* represented the latest achievement in engineering, technology, science, and even the arts. She symbolized progress in mankind's constant quest to create the biggest and best of everything. And that, in turn, gave hope to the common man, because with every new innovation and advancement like the *Titanic,* he believed his life would get better, too. If a ship could be built that not even Mother Nature could sink, surely there would be even more remarkable triumphs that would benefit everyone.

Adding to the allure of the *Titanic* were the more than 1,300 people who booked passages on her maiden voyage. More than half were British, American, and Irish. The rest came from two dozen other countries. The passenger list covered all segments of society: In first class, wealthy industrialists, businessmen, and upper-crust families returning home from European vacations; in second class, young professionals and tradesmen seeking their fortune in America; and in third class, poor immigrants hoping for a better life in the New World. The ship was transporting more than just people. She was carrying their dreams and ambitions.

Out on the open sea, the ship handled beautifully, slicing through the water at near her top speed. On Sunday, April 14, the wireless operator began receiving reports from other ships of icebergs west of the westbound *Titanic.* Later that night, a lookout from the crow's nest spotted an iceberg directly ahead. He immediately alerted the bridge, but the ship couldn't turn fast enough.

Her starboard side brushed up against the iceberg.

The impact buckled a 300-foot-long section of the hull below the waterline, allowing seawater to pour into the forward compartments, weighing down her bow. Despite watertight doors, water soon rushed over the tops of bulkheads, flooding adjoining compartments in much the same way water flows in a tilted ice cube tray. An inspection of the damage by officers revealed a devastating certainty: The ship would sink within a few short hours.

At 12:05 A.M.—about 20 minutes after the collision—Captain Edward J. Smith ordered the crew to prepare the lifeboats and muster the passengers. They had to abandon ship.

Although the *Titanic* seemed to have everything that money could buy, she was lacking in one critical necessity—enough lifeboats. She carried 14 standard-sized lifeboats; two smaller emergency boats, called *cutters*; and four collapsible boats that had pull-up canvas sides. Filled to capacity, the lifeboats could hold 1,178 people—which was slightly more than half the number of people on board. And yet the 20 lifeboats were more than the British Board of Trade Regulations required at the time.

While the boats were being prepared, the wireless operator was sending out calls for help. The nearest vessel to respond, the passenger steamship *Carpathia*, was 58 miles southeast of the stricken ship. That was four hours away, which meant she wouldn't arrive in time.

On the port side of the *Titanic*, the crew let mostly women and children in the lifeboats along with a few men to handle the oars. Husbands and fathers kissed wives and kids and gallantly helped them into the boats before waving good-bye. On the starboard side, men assisted in the loading, but then were allowed to board if no women were seen nearby. Mystifyingly, many boats were launched only half full. In a few instances, male passengers tried to rush a boat only to be repelled when officers pulled out revolvers and fired warning shots in the air. Money, clout, or fame meant nothing in the lifeboats. Rich, fashionable women clad in furs sat side by side with poverty-stricken immigrants in nightclothes.

By 2 A.M., the bow was fully submerged, and the stern was completely out of the water. The vessel was not only listing to port but angling downward so steeply that screaming people were sliding, falling, or jumping into the icy water. From within the ship came a thunderous roar as everything not bolted down crashed forward—grand pianos, tables and chairs, pots and pans, steamer trunks, china and glassware, tons of coal, anchor chains. And then everything that *was* bolted down broke loose—including the ship's boilers, the newfangled ice-making machine, the revolutionary turbine.

The *Titanic* shuddered from a few muffled explosions and then, with a loud cracking sound, she split in two between the third and fourth funnels at 2:18 A.M. The bow quickly sank, but the stern rose until it was nearly vertical. Then, with people clinging to benches, railings, and ventilators, the stern began to plunge, picking up speed downward until it, too, disappeared beneath the surface.

An untold number of passengers and crewmembers were now struggling in the frigid 28-degree water, begging, pleading, crying for help. But few lifeboats came to their aid out of fear of being swamped or capsized. And so one by one, nearly 1,500 poor souls took their last breath, most dying of hypothermia—loss of body heat.

The *Carpathia* arrived shortly after 4 A.M. and began picking up all those lucky enough to have been in a lifeboat. The wealthy lost their valuables and money—things that could be replaced with insurance. The poor lost everything they owned but the clothes on their backs. And many lost husbands or fathers.

Once the massive loss of life became clear, the White Star Line chartered the cable ship CS *Mackay-Bennett* from Halifax, Nova Scotia, to retrieve bodies. She and other ships eventually recovered 333. The remaining victims were never found.

Death cared little about wealth or poverty. The

casualty list included the names of the rich and famous as well as the poor and little known. However, first- and second-class passengers had easier access to the lifeboats than third-class passengers did. More than 60 percent of those in first class were rescued compared with 42 percent from second class and only 25 percent in third class. Just 24 percent of the crew survived. Of the men on board, 20 percent lived compared to 75 percent of the women.

Children didn't fare well. There were 195 unmarried passengers between the ages of 10 weeks and 17 years old. Only 86—less than half—lived. Of the 13 in first class, 11 survived; of 34 in second class, 30 survived; of 134 in third class, only 44 survived. The youngest victim was four months old. Entire families perished. Among them: John and Annie Sage and their nine children, ranging in age from five to twenty, who had left their home in England looking for a fresh start in Jacksonville, Florida; Margaret Rice and her five chil- dren, ages two to ten, who were returning to Spokane, Washington; and Swedish farmers Anders and Alfrida Andersson and their five children, ages two to eleven, who were on their way to Canada. The Sages, Rices, and Anderssons were all in third class.

Among the crew, there were 18 persons between the ages of 14 and 17 working as bellboys and assistants in the kitchen. Only one, 17-year-old assistant cook John

Collins, survived when he swam to an overturned life-boat after he was swept overboard moments before the ship went down.

News of the disaster struck at the hearts of those who lost loved ones and friends. It also rattled those who had an unshakable confidence in progress. Shattered was their belief that the newest and greatest accomplishment meant society was a step closer to perfection. How was it possible, they wondered, that the most magnificent, best-engineered ship ever built could end up at the bottom of the ocean—and on her maiden voyage, no less!

Some good did come out of the tragedy. Following hearings by the United States Senate Inquiry and the British Wreck Commissioner's Inquiry, woefully outdated safety regulations were upgraded. Passenger ships were required to carry more lifeboats and have the wireless radio manned 24 hours a day.

For more than 70 years, the wreckage of the *Titanic* rested untouched and unseen somewhere on the bottom of the North Atlantic. All attempts to find her remains failed until September 1, 1985, when a joint American–French expedition of the Woods Hole Oceanographic Institution, led by Dr. Robert Ballard, and the Institute of France for the Research and Exploration of the Sea, led by Jean-Louis Michel, located the wreck using side-scan sonar. She was found at a depth of nearly 2.5 miles,

370 miles southeast of Mistaken Point, Newfoundland. The unmanned submarine *Argo* captured the first pictures of the *Titanic*'s debris field, including the bow and the stern, which were more than a third of a mile away from each other.

The following year, Dr. Ballard returned to the site aboard *Atlantis II* to conduct the first manned dives to the wreck in the submarine *Alvin*. Debris—pieces of the ship, furniture, dinnerware, and personal items— was scattered over a one-square-mile area. Materials such as wood, carpet, and human remains had disintegrated or been consumed by ocean microbes. Dr. Ballard and his team did not retrieve any artifacts, because they considered it grave robbing. However, in 1994, after years of court challenges, a company called RMS *Titanic*, Inc. was awarded ownership and salvaging rights to the shipwreck. About 6,000 artifacts have since been removed from the wreck, many of which are on display at the National Maritime Museum in Greenwich, England, in the Titanic Museums in Branson, Missouri, and Pigeon Forge, Tennessee, and in traveling exhibits.

Although the sea tragedy happened way back in 1912, the public has never lost its fascination for the world's most famous ship—the RMS *Titanic*.

"Is the *Titanic* Doomed?"

Edith Brown

The idea that the *Titanic* was fated for disaster never crossed Edith Brown's mind. Such a notion seemed ridiculous to the 15-year-old South African. But that disturbing thought did occur to her on the third day of the voyage.

It happened while Edith and her mother, Elizabeth, were each reading a book in the ship's second-class library. A strange middle-aged woman walked over and struck up a conversation with Elizabeth. Edith paid her little attention until the woman said, "There's something about this ship that I find unsettling."

Putting down her book, Edith was now all ears. Elizabeth, who by nature was a nervous person, cast an anxious glance toward Edith before asking the woman, "In what way?"

"Quite frankly, I can't put my finger on it. But when we were in Queenstown, I felt kind of panicky. I wanted my husband to cancel the remainder of the voyage and get me off."

The woman said that she and her husband had crossed the Atlantic several times before, but this was the first time she had ever felt this tense. "Since I've been on the ship, I haven't slept a wink. I have been feeling uneasy the whole time."

Knowing how natural it was to become jittery herself, Elizabeth decided to end the conversation, telling the woman, "I do hope you get a good night's sleep and settle down a bit as the trip goes on." Then Elizabeth returned to her book.

After the woman, whom neither saw again, left the library, Edith said, "Well, that was odd."

She immediately thought of the disturbing moment during the boarding when she, her mother, and her father, Thomas, were walking up the gangway of the *Titanic* in Southampton. Thomas suddenly became faint. His legs began to buckle, forcing him to grab the railing to keep from falling. "What on earth is the matter, Tom?" Elizabeth said, rushing to his aid.

"I don't know, my dear," he replied, wiping his brow.

"You're shaking, and you're pale as a ghost!"

To Edith, it looked as though he had *seen* a ghost.

After taking a few deep breaths, he stood up and said, "I think I'm over it now." His legs steady again, he motioned to Elizabeth and Edith, "Let's get on board."

Here in the library, Edith wondered out loud, "Is it possible Father had the same kind of premonition as that lady when we boarded?"

"I shouldn't tell you this because I don't want you to worry," Elizabeth said, "but Father admitted to me later that he was overcome with a feeling that something bad was going to happen." She nervously tapped her fingers on her book. "Should we be worried?"

Edith shook her head. "Nothing is going to happen. This ship is unsinkable."

She didn't dare tell her mother what Thomas had said on the day of departure when the *Titanic* nearly collided with another ship. As the *Titanic* was leaving the narrow channel in the harbor of Southampton, it moved past the American liner *New York*, which was moored alongside another ship. The suction of the triple-propeller *Titanic* was so powerful that the hawsers of the SS *New York* snapped off, causing dockworkers to flee to avoid getting hit by the dangerous flying ends of the mooring ropes. The only hawser that didn't break was the one holding the bow. The stern of the *New York* swung out toward the port side of the *Titanic*. In the nick of time, tugboats moved into position and nudged the *New York* just enough so that the *Titanic* cleared the stern of the ship by only a few feet. After the close call, Edith's father muttered to her, "This is a bad omen."

He also wasn't pleased that the *Titanic* had departed behind schedule, claiming, "A ship leaving late spells bad luck."

Thinking about her family's history, Edith wondered if her father said that because of what had happened to his brother. Years earlier, Thomas's brother had captained a ship that sank at sea in a tragedy that took his life.

Then there was the bizarre incident mentioned by 12-year-old Robertha "Bertha" Watt, a fellow second-class passenger. On the afternoon of the *Titanic*'s departure, Bertha had accompanied her mother to tea with several ladies. A woman at the table practiced the ancient art of reading tea leaves—a belief that the pattern made by the tea leaves at the bottom of a finished cup can tell the future of the tea drinker. After studying the empty cup of one of the ladies for several minutes, the tea leaf reader shook her head and admitted, "This is strange. I can't see anything. It's like there's just a blank wall and nothing beyond."

Is the Titanic doomed? Edith wondered. She immediately pushed such an unpleasant thought from her mind. After all, this was the most thrilling time of her young life. She and her parents had left their home in Cape Town, South Africa, with plans to create a new life in Seattle, Washington.

Her 60-year-old father, Thomas, was a well-respected

investor and owner of several hotels in South Africa. Sporting a bushy mustache and always looking dapper, he was 20 years older than Elizabeth, a sweet-natured woman devoted to family and friends. Edith's parents doted on her, especially after her younger sister, Dorothy, died in 1908 at the age of eight from diphtheria.

Edith, who looked much younger than her age because she was short and slender, was given the best education possible. She and her parents often traveled to London to shop for clothes for themselves and fixtures for Thomas's hotels.

Encouraged by Elizabeth's sister Josephine, who lived in Seattle, the Browns decided to move there so Thomas could operate a new hotel. In February 1912, Edith and her parents sailed to England and spent several weeks in London, where Thomas booked second-class passage on the *Titanic*. For his American venture, Thomas bought linens, tableware, china, furnishings, and hotel equipment, which were put in the ship's cargo hold. Meanwhile, Edith and her mother went sightseeing and shopping. They bought the latest fashions, including full-length wool coats with velvet cuffs and lapels; feathered and wide-brimmed hats; and button-up leather boots.

The rest of their worldly possessions were kept in Thomas's leather Gladstone bag—a cross between a small suitcase and a large briefcase. The bag held

16

cash, jewelry, gold coins, and important documents. Thomas also wore a money belt, which hid cash in a concealed compartment, and had gold coins sewn in his formal vests and in the hems of the women's coats. In those days, it was considered the safest way to travel with money.

Edith had never seen her parents in such high spirits. She, too, was caught up in the happy anticipation of the *Titanic*'s maiden voyage and a promising future in America. Her brain whirled with questions about the trip. *Will I get to wear all the pretty dresses Mother and Father bought me? Will I meet people my own age on the ship? Will there be dancing? Will I like Seattle? Will I make friends? Will I go to school or work in Father's hotel?* She could hardly wait to live out the answers.

The Browns took the train from London directly to the Southampton Docks, where Edith got her first glimpse of the *Titanic*. "It's so big and beautiful!" she marveled.

The ship's white superstructure towered above its massive black hull. Wisps of smoke curled out of three of its four buff-colored black-tipped funnels as the morning sun lit up the brass-ringed portholes. Baggage carts, supply wagons, and cargo containers were pushed and pulled into position while cranes lowered freight into the holds. Early-arriving passengers were already on the top deck (called the Boat Deck), leaning against the railing and waving to well-wishers below. Porters were scurrying up and down the three gangways, carrying boxes, packages, and flowers.

As Edith and her parents headed up the passenger gangway, her mounting excitement was interrupted by Thomas's near fainting spell. Once he recovered, they hurried to their cabins. To save money, Edith and her mother shared a cabin on E Deck while Thomas shared a single bunk-bed cabin with a male passenger. Edith took the top bunk, which, like the others, had curtains for privacy, big white pillows, and crisp white sheets under a bedspread with the White Star logo in the center.

Over the next few days, Edith made new friends but spent most of the time curled up with a good book in the wood-paneled, well-stocked library.

On Saturday, the fourth day of the voyage, the Browns were lounging outside on deck chairs when the *Titanic*'s 62-year-old captain, Edward John Smith, stopped to chat with them. He looked every bit the part of a captain, dressed in a navy blue jacket adorned with four gold rings around each cuff, sharply creased navy blue pants, and black patent leather shoes.

"Are you enjoying the voyage?" he asked them.

"It has been a most pleasurable experience," Thomas answered.

Turning his attention to Edith, the captain stroked

his thick white beard and asked her, "And how about you, young lady?"

"It's the best ship we've ever been on," she replied.

The captain chuckled and said, "I'm glad to hear that."

Thomas asked, "Is the ship running on schedule?"

"Yes, we are making good time because of the excellent weather so far," the captain replied. "The temperature likely will drop over the next few days but that won't have any effect on arriving in New York on time. And now I must bid you good-bye. Have a pleasant day." He gave a half salute and walked on to talk with other passengers.

The next day, Sunday, the Browns attended church services in the dining saloon but spent the rest of the day belowdecks because it had turned cold outside. Before dinner that evening, the family braved the chill for a quick stroll and admired the beautiful sunset that had turned the glasslike sea a vibrant gold.

At dinner, they engaged in a lively conversation with their regular dining companions, the Reverend Ernest Carter and his wife, Lilian, who were from a small, poor parish near London. For the personable middle-aged couple who had never been to America, this was a long-planned trip of a lifetime, partially paid for by donations from parishioners.

"It's so cold outside," Edith remarked.

"Indeed it is," said Rev. Carter. "A steward told me some of the other ships in the area have reported on the Marconi that they saw ice fields."

"Oh, I hope we see an iceberg," said Edith.

After dinner, the Browns joined about 100 people at a hymn-sing conducted by Rev. Carter in the second-class lounge. He introduced each hymn with a story about its origin. Among the songs was "For Those in Peril on the Sea"—which would soon prove, sadly, to be a fitting choice. At the end of the hymn-sing, Rev. Carter said, "It is the first time that hymns have been sung on this boat, but we trust and pray it won't be the last."

At 10 P.M., Thomas escorted Edith and her mother to their cabin and then went to the smoking lounge. The two fell fast asleep. At 11:40 P.M., they were awakened by a shudder and several bumps.

Edith jumped out of the top berth, opened the port-hole, stuck her head out, and stared into the blackness. The reflection of the lights from the ship danced gently on the calm sea. Looking toward the stern, she noticed the propellers were churning up the water and causing a distinct vibration that caused glasses on the wash-stand to clink and the cabin to squeak and rattle.

"I wonder what that is all about," Elizabeth said.

Minutes later, the vibration stopped and so had the engines. Edith sat next to her mother and said, "Everything seems so quiet."

The silence was broken by a knock on the door. Edith opened it and saw her father, still dressed in his smoking jacket. He told them calmly, "There's talk that the ship has struck an iceberg."

Elizabeth gasped. "Oh, my dear lord!"

Edith stuck her head out of the porthole again but couldn't see any sign of an iceberg or an ice field.

"Let's not get worried, but let's get prepared," Thomas said. "Put on warm clothing and life jackets." He reached on top of the wardrobe and pulled down the two life vests that had been stowed there.

Both women donned warm jumpers and their new topcoats. Thomas helped them with their bulky life jackets, which were made of square chunks of cork held together with stitched canvas that hung over the shoulders and were tied at the waist.

After the women put them on over their heavy clothing, Edith briefly ignored the crisis and giggled. "Oh, Mother, look at us. We're so fat."

Elizabeth wasn't amused. "Tom, where is your life vest?"

"I'll find one later. The important thing is to get you both to the Boat Deck."

On their way up the stairs, Edith saw stewards in the hallways, rapping on doors and calling out, "Everyone up with life vests on, please!"

Arriving at the Boat Deck, the Browns parked

themselves near Lifeboat 14, which was still covered and fastened to the davits. Passengers milled around in various attire, displaying different reactions. Some were clad in nightclothes, others in formal wear. Some were fretting, others were joking. Elizabeth was one of those fretting.

Stomping her feet to keep warm, Edith asked her father, "It's so cold out here. How soon before we can get back to our warm cabin?"

"Be patient. It won't be long before I'll be tucking you both into bed."

Edith noticed he hadn't looked her in the eye. She figured he said that for the benefit of her whimpering mother.

Seamen were busy preparing the lifeboats for lowering. Fifth Officer Harold Lowe, who was in charge of filling and launching several lifeboats nearby, yelled at his crew, "Get a bloody move on!"

Edith curled both her arms tightly around her father's arm as people were being helped into the first boats.

Because the ship had built up a good head of steam before the collision, the pressure had to be vented to prevent the boilers from exploding. With safety valves open, steam blasted out of the waste pipes at the top of the funnels, causing a constant ear-shattering roar that drowned out virtually all other sound. Officers, crewmembers, and passengers communicated with hand signals or shouted through cupped hands.

The blaring noise made some passengers cower in fear, thinking the ship was about to explode. Women covered the ears of their children with their hands or shawls. Several people crouched or clung to each other. Elizabeth clutched her husband's hand and burst into tears.

After about a half hour, about 1 A.M., the constant blast began to diminish. Once again people were able to hear each other. The ship's band, made up of eight musicians, had moved from the first-class lounge to the Boat Deck and was playing the most popular waltzes and ragtime tunes of the day to keep the passengers' spirits up, not that they were paying much attention to it.

"Women and children first!" hollered Lowe. "The rest of you stand well back away from the lifeboat!"

Men pushed their loved ones toward the front of unlaunched boats so they would be next in line.

Elizabeth cried out in alarm, "Oh, Thomas, there aren't enough lifeboats to handle all the people!"

"Now, now, Elizabeth," Thomas said soothingly. "You'd be surprised how many people these boats can hold."

Edith knew he was lying solely to calm her mother. Edith had done the math. The ship had only 20 lifeboats, most with a capacity of 65 people. There were more than 2,200 people on board. Her mother was right—there weren't nearly enough boats for everyone, and that frightened Edith. Still, the girl tried not to show how afraid she was.

As Edith watched men assist women and children into lifeboats, Rev. Carter and his wife, Lilian, joined the Browns and tried to comfort them, saying that everything would turn out just fine. Lilian chose to stay with her husband rather than go into a lifeboat.

"Come on, ladies!" a crewman urged Edith and her mother. "Quick as you can!"

Edith was dreading the moment when she would have to leave her father. As she and her weeping mother were pushed into Lifeboat 14, Elizabeth pleaded to Thomas, "Get into another boat, Tom! Go around to the other side!"

Hearing her mother sob and looking at her somber father, Edith could no longer keep from crying. She stifled an outburst but let the tears stream down her face while she clenched her hands on her lap.

Officer Lowe and three other crewmen got in the boat, which began its descent. Thomas made no effort to leave his spot. He just stood there, gently puffing on his cigar, never taking his eyes off of the two most important people in his life. As No. 14 was lowered down the ship's side in slow, jerky movements, Edith shouted at him, "Do what Mother says! Please, Father, find another boat!"

Thomas gave them both a little wave and blew them a kiss. He leaned over the railing and shouted down to them, "I'll see you in New York!"

Now Edith was sobbing. She knew full well that the situation was near hopeless for those left behind.

On the way down, Edith saw through the lighted portholes people still in their cabins, grabbing valuables and other possessions. Just before reaching the water, the bow of the lifeboat stopped descending while the stern continued to go down. The falls had jammed, causing the boat to tip backward at a dangerous angle. Women screamed as they tumbled into each other. Once the boat was released from the falls, it slammed into the water, drenching the passengers in an icy bath.

When No. 14 moved far enough away from the sinking *Titanic*, the seamen rested their oars. All eyes were locked on the dying ship, its bow almost completely submerged, its stern slowly rising out of the water.

Rocking back and forth in anguish, Elizabeth kept moaning, "Tom, oh, Tom!"

Edith gripped her mother's arm and said, "Father is a smart man. He probably found a way to get in another boat."

"Oh, dear God, I hope so. But he wasn't wearing

a life jacket!" She buried her head in her hands and wailed.

Edith could still hear the band, which had switched to playing hymns. She was surprised to see lights shining from the portholes that were now underwater. What tugged at her heart the most was helplessly watching people scamper toward the rising stern in a desperate bid to gain a few precious minutes of life before they met almost certain death.

The music soon quit and was replaced by shrieks on deck, crashing crockery and glass from inside, and thunderous noises of loosened machinery slamming into bulkheads deep within the hull.

Edith and her mother put their hands over their ears to block out the sounds of human suffering, but their eyes remained trained on the unimaginable scene in front of them. The foremost funnel toppled over amid a cloud of steam, smoke, and sparks. The vessel split in two, shuddered from huge underwater explosions, and then, accompanied by loud gurgling and bubbling, disappeared, leaving behind a slight mist.

There was little anyone in No. 14 could say. They were all too stunned, too weary, too cold.

Throughout the night, all the lifeboats drifted in a three-square-mile area in near silence except for the occasional sob, cough, or whimper. When dawn broke a few hours later, Edith quaked at the ghastly scene.

As far as the eye could see, gray bodies—many in life vests—were bobbing in upright positions. She saw corpses of women and children still clinging to each other and frozen bodies sprawled on floating debris and deck chairs that had been tied together.

Edith and her mother remained cuddled together until the rescue ship *Carpathia* arrived and began picking up the survivors. When it was No. 14's turn, some women climbed the Jacob's ladder; others, like Edith and Elizabeth, were brought on board by a boatswain's chair. The youngest children were hauled up in small mailbags.

Edith and Elizabeth could barely stand because they had no feeling in their legs and feet. But they forced themselves to walk until circulation returned to their limbs. They went looking for Thomas and were worried sick that he wasn't on any of the earlier lifeboats. Every time another lifeboat reached the *Carpathia*, Edith and her mother, like most other survivors, rushed to the ship's railing, hoping to spot their loved ones.

When the last survivors were brought aboard, Edith and her mother were devastated that Thomas wasn't among them. "There's still a chance Father could have been picked up by another ship that hasn't reported the good news," Edith said. "Let's not give up hope until we reach New York and learn about other possible survivors."

"We're clutching at straws, but what choice do we have?" sighed Elizabeth.

"I want to believe that Father will be there on the wharf, waiting for us."

But in their hearts, they knew he was dead. Every night in the *Carpathia*'s main lounge, where they slept, the two wept over Thomas's fate. In their time of grief, they were moved by the extraordinary compassion shown to the survivors by the *Carpathia*'s passengers and crew, who tried to make them as comfortable as possible, given the circumstances. Passengers donated clothes and, in some cases, even turned their cabins over to the survivors. The poorest third-class immigrant and the wealthiest first-class passenger received equal attention.

Hours before the *Carpathia* docked in New York, Elizabeth had a heart-to-heart talk with Edith. "My dear, you're old enough that I can confide in you some harsh truths," Elizabeth said. "Our money and our valuables were in Father's Gladstone bag, which was locked in the safe of the purser's office. It's now at the bottom of the ocean. All the things Father bought for the new hotel were not insured. Even if, by some miracle, Father is alive, we're still broke. And if our worst fears are realized and he didn't survive, we no longer have any visible means of support."

"What will we do, Mother?"

"We must continue on to Seattle because we don't know anyone else in America. And besides, your aunt Josephine is expecting us."

"What will we do for money?"

"Our new coats are worth more than you think."

"What do you mean?"

"After we bought them, Father had several gold sovereigns sewn in the hems for safekeeping. We'll have enough to live on until we get back on our feet."

When the *Carpathia* arrived in New York, the wharves were crammed with thousands of spectators, curiosity seekers, and loved ones. Amid a blaze of camera flashes, reporters and photographers squeezed around the gangway, firing rapid-fire questions to the survivors: "Did you see dead bodies in the water?" "How did you survive?" "Did you lose all your money?"

The first-class passengers, surrounded by shore personnel, left the ship first and were whisked away in taxis or their private limousines. The second-class passengers disembarked next. As the crowd surged forward, Edith and Elizabeth were inadvertently shoved around until several burly policemen cleared a path for them. The women were put under the care of the Women's Junior League of New York.

Taken to a hostel, they had their first hot bath in days. Never had a long soak in the tub felt so good. The next day, though, brought heartache. There were no reports of any more survivors. Mother and daughter would never see Thomas again. After accepting that cold reality, there was nothing else Elizabeth could tell Edith except, "It's just you and me now."

Thomas Brown's body was never recovered.

Rev. Ernest Carter and his wife, Lilian, also perished, and their bodies were never recovered, either.

Edith and her mother traveled to Seattle, but they didn't stay long and returned to South Africa. They were relieved to learn that Thomas had left them various stocks and bonds worth a tidy sum. Elizabeth remarried and moved to Southern Rhodesia (now Zimbabwe). Because she didn't get along with her stepfather, Edith lived with family friends in Johannesburg.

In 1917, at the age of 20, she married Frederick Haisman, a shipbuilder's draftsman who loved to sail. While living most of their married lives in South Africa and then in Southampton, they raised ten children. The couple was married for 60 years until Frederick's death in 1977.

Ten years later, more than 2,000 items were retrieved from the wreck of the Titanic. One of the items was believed to be Thomas's gold watch, which was found in a Gladstone bag along with $60,000—all claimed by the salvage company.

Edith lived to be 100 years old, leaving behind 40

grandchildren and great-grandchildren and outliving four of her children.

About five months before her death, Edith—the Titanic survivor who lived to be the oldest—set sail on her final ocean voyage, a memorial expedition aboard the Island Breeze. On September 1, 1996, the ship stopped at 41°46′ N, 50°14′ W in the North Atlantic—two and a half miles above the Titanic's remains—and held a memorial service for the 1,502 souls who perished 84 years earlier. As a lone piper played, Edith was helped to the ship's railing, where she dropped a wreath into the water. At last she had fulfilled one of her life's goals—to properly say a final farewell to her father. As memories of that horrible night came flooding back to her, she wept. The Island Breeze then blew its whistle three times in a traditional salute to a departed ship.

(Her son David Haisman, of Southampton, wrote a book about her life called Titanic, The Edith Brown Story, from which material was used for this story. For further information about the book, contact Haisman at titanicanme@aol.com.)

"I'm Not Dead Yet"

John B. "Jack" Thayer III

Jack Thayer looked over the side of the sinking *Titanic* and stared into the frigid black sea. He knew he had to jump. But he just couldn't do it. Not yet. Plunging into water so cold it could make one's heart stop was his only hope, which wasn't much. *I'm probably going to die*, he thought. *But what choice do I have?*

It wasn't supposed to end this way for 17-year-old John B. "Jack" Thayer III. His life had been scripted from the day he was born into a wealthy family from Haverford, Pennsylvania. His father, John, was a vice president of the Pennsylvania Railroad, and his mother, Marian, who was raising four children, had come from a prominent family. Jack's childhood thrived from everything that wealth and privilege could bestow on a kid—a mansion staffed by servants and maids, private schools with the best athletic coaches, and European vacations at the finest resorts.

His father had Jack's future all planned out. Upon graduation from Haverford School, Jack would attend Princeton and then live in London, Paris, Berlin, or Vienna, where he would apprentice with the sharpest minds in international banking. Then he would return to the United States and begin a lucrative career in high finance. Yes, his future was all planned out. Facing death on a sinking ship was not part of the plan.

Jack, his parents, and his mother's maid, Margaret Fleming, had enjoyed a fun-filled vacation in Europe and were returning home aboard the *Titanic*. They were among more than 300 first-class passengers spoiled by the white-gloved service of hundreds of stewards and stewardesses at their beck and call.

Jack occupied a spacious wood-paneled stateroom next door to his parents on C Deck. Instead of a small porthole, his room featured a full window. Like all first-class accommodations, his stateroom had hot and cold running water, a private bathroom, and an individually controlled heater.

On board, his father introduced Jack to the rich and powerful captains of industry and big business, including one of America's wealthiest men, John Jacob Astor IV. The teenager and his dad also mingled with the very people most responsible for building the world's greatest ship—Thomas Andrews, one of the *Titanic*'s designers; Anthony "Archie" Frost, the builder's chief engineer; and J. Bruce Ismay, chairman and managing director of the White Star Line, which owned the ship. Impressed by his intelligence, charm, and manners, the men often included Jack in their daily discussions.

On Sunday, April 14, Jack spent most of the sunny but brisk day walking on the Promenade Deck with his parents, stopping for brief chats with Andrews and Ismay. Later that afternoon, as the temperatures began to drop rapidly, Ismay showed the Thayers a wireless message that had been received a few hours earlier from the SS *Baltic,* a ship a few hundred miles west of the *Titanic*. It read, in part: "Captain Smith, *Titanic*—Have had moderate, variable winds and clear, fine weather since leaving. Greek steamer *Athenai* reports passing icebergs and large quantities of field ice today in lat. 41°51′ N, long. 49°42′ W . . . Wish you and *Titanic* all success. Commander."

"We might see some icebergs and growlers," Ismay told the Thayers.

"What are growlers?" Jack asked.

"Small bergs that have broken off big ones," Ismay answered. "You probably won't spot any today because it will be dark by the time we reach the field ice around nine P.M."

That evening, the Thayers dressed in their finery for dinner. Because his parents were invited to dine with friends in the ship's elegant à la Carte Restaurant, Jack chose to eat alone in the dining saloon. After his meal, he struck up a conversation with Milton Long, son of Judge Charles Long, of Springfield, Massachusetts.

"I've been traveling alone throughout Europe the last few months, and now I'm heading home," said Milton, a strapping, dark-haired young man who looked about Jack's age but was 29. "I was skiing at St. Moritz. Exhilarating. Didn't break any bones although I had my fair share of spills. Also tried bob-sledding. Let me tell you, my friend, flying down a curvy run at blinding speeds can make your life flash before your eyes. Ever try it?"

"No, but I did some skiing a few weeks ago in Switzerland and Austria with my parents. We were also in Holland, Germany, and England on holiday."

Milton, who had attended college but never graduated, said he was a globetrotter in search of a good time. In fact, he had traveled around the world the previous year. Of all his exploits, the most exciting happened on June 29, 1911. He was a passenger aboard the steamer *Spokane* on a voyage through Alaska's Inside Passage when it struck an uncharted rock in Seymour Narrows and was wrecked. Of the 250 passengers aboard, only one perished. "The only time I got my feet wet was when I had to jump from the lifeboat to the shore," Milton told Jack. "The *Spokane* accident is the big reason why I'm on the *Titanic*. I had planned to go home earlier on a different ship. But my father didn't want any more danger to befall me, so he insisted I sail on her because she's unsinkable."

Jack and Milton traded stories about their travel experiences and talked about Jack's favorite hobby—collecting stamps. After more than two hours, they parted company, agreeing to meet in the morning.

Pulling up the collar of his coat to ward off the frosty night air, Jack took a walk on the deck and admired the starlit sky. *I've never seen stars shine brighter*, he thought. *They sparkle like cut diamonds.* A light haze, barely noticeable, hung low over the water. Although he had spent much time on the ocean, he had never seen the sea smoother. *It's a night that makes me feel glad to be alive.*

After saying good night to his parents, he went into his cabin, where he put on pajamas and cracked open the window, allowing in a cool breeze. As he was ready to climb into bed, he felt the ship make a sudden movement to port. The engines stopped, creating an eerie silence except for the breeze whistling through the open window. Soon he heard the distant noise of running feet and muffled voices in the passageway.

Curious, he put on his slippers and heavy overcoat and called out to his parents, "I'm going up on deck and see the fun."

"I'll join you once I get dressed," his father said.

It was freezing cold when Jack reached the deck. He looked around but didn't see anything out of the ordinary except for some small chunks of ice scattered on the starboard side of the forward deck. After his father arrived, Jack stopped a crewmember and asked, "What happened?"

"The ship hit an iceberg," the crewman replied. "Over there." He pointed off the starboard side, but their eyes hadn't adjusted to the darkness, and they couldn't spot it. They soon noticed that the ship was angled slightly toward the bow. Coming in from the cold, the Thayers went into a lounge where several passengers were milling around, not concerned in the least. They were smoking, playing cards, or having a nightcap.

Neither Jack nor his father were worried, believing, as most everyone else did, that the ship was unsinkable. Just then Jack spotted Andrews, Ismay, and several officers hurrying through the lounge. He couldn't help noticing they all looked grim.

Mr. Thayer stopped Andrews and said, "So, my good man, what are we facing here?"

"It's a dire situation," Andrews replied, his face etched in dismay. "The ship is taking on water from a gash in the forward compartments on the starboard side. She doesn't have much more than an hour or two to live." Then Andrews and the others marched out of the lounge.

The news rocked Jack. "I can't believe what I just heard," he said.

"If Andrews said it, it must be true," replied Mr. Thayer. "No one is better qualified to know than the man who helped design the ship."

By 12:15 P.M., the stewards were pounding on the doors of all the cabins, urging passengers to get dressed and put on their life jackets. Jack and his dad rushed back to warn his mother. She and her maid were already fully dressed. Jack scurried into his room and put on two vests, a tweed suit, a life jacket, and over-coat. Then the Thayers and their maid hustled up to the lounge on A Deck, which was rapidly filling with nervous passengers.

Jack's new friend, Milton Long, came over to him and asked, "Mind if I stick with you, old sport?"

"Of course you can," Jack replied.

In the crush of shoving, surging people, Jack lost sight of his parents and the maid. He and Milton searched the lifeboats as they were being lowered but couldn't find them. By now several of the boats had already left the ship.

"They must have gotten in one of the boats," he shouted to Milton above the din of the steam vents.

"What do you think we should do?" Milton yelled back.

Not seeing any more women or children in the

area, Jack said, "Let's see if we can find a lifeboat."

A throng of men was pressing to get into the last two forward starboard boats. He saw Ismay, who earlier had been assisting women and children, hop into Lifeboat C, the last one from that section of the ship.

"It's now every man for himself," Jack told Milton.

They watched two stewards jump into Lifeboat C from the deck above. An officer on the lower deck fired two shots in the air as a warning to anyone else who thought about leaping into the boat. The stewards were ordered out before it was lowered. All that were left were two collapsible boats lashed to the roof of the officers' cabin on the Boat Deck at the foot of the first funnel.

"Shouldn't we fight our way into one of the remaining boats?" Milton asked. "The ship isn't going to stay afloat much longer."

"I don't think we should try it. There's so much confusion, those last two boats might not reach the water right side up."

"Do you think we're going to die?"

Jack shook his head. "I'm not ready yet."

They leaned over the side and watched what they thought were the last lifeboats rowing away from the sinking ship. The sloping deck was now about 40 feet above the surface.

"What are you going to do?" Milton asked.

Seeing the dangling falls that had lowered the life-boats, Jack replied, "I'm going to jump out and catch one of these falls, then slide down into the water and swim to the closest lifeboat."

"Are you daft?" Milton said. "If you jump from here, you might hit a floating steamer chair or wreckage and get knocked unconscious. Besides, the water is below freezing. The cold will kill you within minutes; that is, if you don't drown from the suction when the ship goes under, even if you are wearing a life jacket. Jumping into the water is not a good idea."

"Yes, I guess you are right," Jack said glumly. The two walked over to a sheltered stairway near the second funnel and pondered their next move. The roaring of the exhaust steam had stopped, so now all that could be heard was the band playing hymns and desperate people lamenting their fate.

"If I don't make it, sport, will you please let my parents know that my last thoughts were of them?" Milton said. "And tell them I am ever so grateful for the swell life they provided me."

"If the worse happens to me, let my mother and father know that I love them very much," said Jack.

Neither said anything for the next several minutes, lost in their own thoughts about their mortality. Jack pictured some of the grand times he had enjoyed in his privileged life with his brother, two sisters, and parents, and how good they all had been to him. *Father had everything planned out for me, and it doesn't look like I'm going to live it,* he thought. He felt sorry for his parents and siblings, and how much they would grieve for him. And he felt sorry for himself.

But then Jack snapped out of his self-pitying mood. *I'm not dead yet. As long as I'm still breathing, there's still hope.* "I'm jumping," he announced.

Milton grabbed him by the arm and said, "It's too dangerous. From here it's at least a forty-foot jump."

"We can't stay here. We have no other choice."

Milton sighed. "You're right. But let's wait until the deck is about ten feet from the waterline and then jump so we're less likely to hurt ourselves. That will still give us time to swim away from the suction when the ship goes down."

By 2:15 A.M., the vessel was listing hard to port and taking a sharper angle downward. Water had engulfed the bow and was moving rapidly toward the bridge, forcing the hundreds on deck to scramble toward the rising stern.

"Are you ready to jump and swim for it?" asked Jack, tightening his life jacket.

"Not really," Milton replied. "I'm not a very good swimmer."

"Swim hard. Your life depends on it."

By now, the water was about 12 feet from the deck.

"I guess it's time," said Milton. He shook hands with Jack. "Good luck, sport. Hope to see you in New York." He climbed over the railing and adjusted his life vest. Looking back toward Jack, he asked, "You're coming, aren't you?"

"Go ahead, Milton. I'll be right behind you."

Milton shouted, "Here goes!" He slid down the tilted starboard side of the ship, facing the hull.

Jack whipped off his overcoat, sat on the railing, and counted down from five. Then, facing out, he pushed off with his hands and feet and jumped as far away from the ship as he could. When he hit the water, the shock of the cold sucked the breath out of his lungs. He plunged under the surface, spinning and tumbling from the suction of the sinking ship. Battling with all his might, he flailed away, refusing his brain's orders to breathe. He had only seconds left to reach the surface before his lungs would force open his mouth and nose.

Just when he thought he couldn't hold his breath for another second, Jack burst through the surface and gulped air—but it was so cold that his lungs burned. The 28-degree water made his entire body feel as though he had been stabbed by a thousand knives. Trying to block the horrible discomfort from his mind, Jack swam hard. When he was about 40 yards away, he stopped and treaded water. He looked around for Milton but couldn't find him.

If Jack was to survive, he had only a few minutes to get out of the water before hypothermia would set in. Rather than swim toward the nearest lifeboat—wherever that was—he gazed in utter fascination at the final moments of the *Titanic*. Its lights still shone and the band still played, even though the front third of the ship was below the surface. As the water washed over the base of the first funnel, more boilers were breaking free from their moorings and exploding. On the decks, the doomed huddled by the rising stern. Suddenly, the ship buckled and, with the most horrendous wrenching sound Jack had ever heard, it split in two.

The second funnel—large enough for two automobiles to pass through side by side—toppled over and, in a shower of sparks and steam, slammed into the water about ten yards from Jack. The suction from the impact pulled him under, and once again he fought his way toward the surface. Putting his hand above his head to push away any obstruction, Jack brushed up against Lifeboat B, which was floating upside down with its hull out of the water. Four men were clinging to the exposed keel. Jack pulled himself up as far as he could, but with no feeling in his legs and totally exhausted from his struggles, he couldn't get all the way onto the hull. "Please, can you help me?" he begged, holding out his hand. Someone gripped it and pulled him up.

The *Titanic*'s stern continued its steady rise into the

air until it reached a 70-degree angle. To the horror of those on Lifeboat B, their tiny craft was sucked toward the sinking stern until they were almost underneath the propellers. "It's going to come down right on top of us!" Jack shouted. But then the stern slid beneath the surface with hardly any suction.

The *Titanic* was no more.

About a minute passed in almost dead silence. Then Jack heard calls for help. Dozens turned into hundreds, gradually swelling into a horrible wailing chant from those left thrashing in the deadly water. The ghastly sound—which lasted about 20 minutes before fading away—reminded him of the locusts in the summer Pennsylvania woods.

Jack knew that several lifeboats had plenty of room and were only a few hundred yards away, and yet they hadn't returned to help. *How could any human being fail to heed these cries?* Jack wondered. *How can they live with themselves?*

A few survivors, including Second Officer Charles Lightoller, managed to swim to the overturned lifeboat. Jack and the others hauled them out until more than 20 passengers and crewmen—all male—covered every square inch of the hull, which was riding extremely low in the water. They were sitting, kneeling, and lying in uncomfortable positions, holding on to the half-inch overlaps of the hull's planking.

For hours nobody dared change position, worried that a sudden movement could tilt the exposed hull and pitch them into the sea. The calm water grew a little choppier, and occasionally a small wave would wash over them, coating the hull in a thin layer of ice. Adding to their woes, the buoyant air was gradually leaking from under the overturned craft, lowering the hull farther into the water. They kept trying to hail the other lifeboats, but either the people didn't hear them or wouldn't answer.

To pass the time, the men prayed and sang hymns. There was nothing else they could do but hang on and hope that their boat would stay afloat long enough for them to be rescued.

Shortly before 4 A.M., they saw the masthead light of the *Carpathia* pop up over the horizon and creep toward them. "We'll be saved, lads!" someone shouted.

But because it was still dark and the *Carpathia* was in an ice field, it moved agonizingly slow. At dawn the men on Lifeboat B saw the rescue ship, which was still a few miles away, hoisting aboard survivors from other lifeboats.

With rescue so close at hand, Jack feared that their overturned craft would sink before the *Carpathia* reached them. A breeze had kicked up, making it rock and causing more air to seep out from underneath. It was sinking lower by the minute.

The men untangled themselves until they all could stand, except for Harold Bride, the assistant wireless operator, whose legs were too numb to move. To maintain the craft's buoyancy, Lightoller made them line up in two rows facing the bow. Then as the hull rocked with the waves, he shouted, "All together, lean to the left" or "Lean to the right." By moving in unison, they kept the boat fairly level. But several men, including Jack, had to hang on to Bride to keep him from slipping off. They also had to hold on to the body of the chief wireless operator, Jack Phillips, who perished during the night.

About 6:30 A.M., Lightoller found the whistle he thought he had lost and blew it until he attracted the attention of other lifeboats. Two boats—No. 4 and No. 12—rowed over to the craft. Half the men from Lifeboat B transferred over to No. 4. One of the women in No. 4 was Jack's mother, who was so exhausted from helping row for four hours that she didn't recognize him. He did not spot her as he hopped into No. 12.

After everyone was off Lifeboat B, the sun peeked over the horizon, bathing the sea in a golden glow. It was the most beautiful sunrise Jack had ever seen, and he lifted his face so he could feel the first rays of the sun. Closing his eyes, he smiled and thought, *I'm saved! I'm going to live!*

The *Carpathia* continued to collect the survivors

from all the other lifeboats until finally No. 12—the last one—got its turn. Although he was numb from the cold, Jack had enough strength in his hands and legs to climb the Jacob's ladder.

When Jack planted his feet on the deck, one of the first people he spotted was his mother. He let out a loud whoop of joy.

"Oh, dear God, you're alive!" she exclaimed, hugging her son. "I knew that this was the last lifeboat, and I was so afraid that if you and your father weren't on it, I'd just fall to pieces." With darting eyes, she looked over Jack's shoulder and asked, "Where's your father?"

Jack's stomach twisted in a knot. "I thought he was with you, Mother. I haven't seen him since we were separated."

Mrs. Thayer's joy turned to instant grief. She covered her mouth and began to shake. Grabbing her to keep her from collapsing, he led her to a chair and held her as she sobbed. He tried to maintain a brave front, but his sorrow unleashed his own tears.

After Jack gained his composure, a crewmember handed him a cup of coffee laced with brandy. It was the first alcoholic drink Jack had ever tasted. It warmed him but burned his throat and stomach.

A *Carpathia* passenger loaned him a pair of pajamas and told him to nap in his bunk bed. Jack stripped off his wet, half-frozen clothes, which were taken away to be dried. Then he fell into a deep sleep for three hours. When he woke up, he donned his dried clothes and walked around the deck.

The *Carpathia*'s captain, Arthur Rostron, turned his cabin over to three newly widowed first-class passengers—Jack's mother, Mrs. George Widener, and Mrs. John Jacob Astor. Jack slept on the floor of their stateroom every night.

The four-day voyage to New York was shrouded in heartache and misery. Although more than 700 survivors were grateful to be alive, virtually everyone was grieving over the loss of a spouse, parent, child, relative, or friend. It was still hard to fathom that more than twice as many died as were saved.

Jack tried to come to terms with his father's death, but it wasn't easy. There were times during the day when he wanted to think of anything else. But no matter where he went or what he did on the *Carpathia*, he encountered people in mourning—especially the widows—and that triggered his own sorrow.

Survivor J. Bruce Ismay, head of the company that owned the *Titanic*, was so traumatized by the tragedy that he refused to leave his cabin. About six hours before the *Carpathia*'s arrival into New York Harbor, the ship's doctor approached Jack and asked him to talk to Ismay. "He's in a terrible state of mind," the doctor said. "He won't eat or sleep or talk to anyone. He is simply too distraught."

"What makes you think I can do anything for him?" Jack asked.

"Ismay hasn't responded to adults. I hear that you are a levelheaded, smart lad, and that he took a shine to you and your family. Perhaps seeing a young face and hearing a young voice will help relieve some of his paralyzing shock."

"Sure, I'll give it a whirl," said Jack.

Jack knocked on Ismay's door. Not getting a response, he walked in. When Jack had last seen him, Ismay was dressed in his finest evening clothes with his gray-speckled black hair neatly combed and his dark flowing mustache perfectly trimmed. He was the epitome of male elegance.

Now Jack was gazing at a shell of a man, an emotional wreck. Clad in pajamas, Ismay was slumped on the edge of his bed, staring straight ahead and trembling. He hadn't shaved in days. What stunned Jack the most was Ismay's hair. To Jack, it looked like it had turned whitish-gray overnight.

"Hello, Mr. Ismay. It's me, Jack Thayer."

Ismay didn't acknowledge him in any way and silently continued to look ahead with a fixed stare.

But Jack didn't stop trying to reach out to him. "Sir, this was a terrible, terrible accident. It's not your fault. There were many brave crewmen who did everything in their power to save lives, even at the cost of their own. You should be proud of them." Despite no reaction from Ismay, Jack kept talking. "I saw how you helped women and children in the lifeboats. You had a perfect right to get in the last boat. No one can fault you for that."

Nothing Jack said could bring any response from Ismay. Jack finally gave up and left Ismay exactly as he found him—a devastated man.

Jack told himself that despite his own heartache, he had to remain strong for his mother's sake. He also understood that he had been given a second chance at life, and he wanted to make the most of it in honor of his father. *After all,* he thought, *I have a plan to follow.*

The body of Jack Thayer's father, John B. Thayer Sr., was never found. Milton Long's body was the 126th corpse recovered by the search ship Mackay-Bennett. *He was buried in his hometown of Springfield, Massachusetts.*

Jack's mother, Marian, never remarried. Having inherited a large sum from her husband and parents, she remained in Haverford, Pennsylvania, until her death on April 14, 1944—the 32nd anniversary of the Titanic *striking the iceberg. She was 71.*

Jack graduated from the University of Pennsylvania and went into the banking business. He later became the financial vice president and treasurer of his alma mater. He and his wife, Lois, raised two sons, Edward C. Thayer and John B. Thayer IV.

Edward was killed in World War II.

In 1940, Jack wrote The Sinking of the SS *Titanic*, a booklet recalling his experiences on that fateful voyage. Some material from that booklet was used in this story. Jack died in 1945 at the age of 50.

After the disaster, J. Bruce Ismay was the target of withering criticism—some of it unjustified—from the American and British press for deserting the ship while women and children were still on board. Newspapers called him "J. Brute Ismay" and suggested changing the color of the White Star Line flag to yellow. London society shunned Ismay and labeled him one of the biggest cowards in history. He also faced unproven accusations that he pressured the captain to keep the ship's speed up as it entered iceberg territory so that the Titanic might arrive ahead of schedule.

Because of the tragedy, Ismay announced that all ships owned by his company would carry enough lifeboats to accommodate all passengers. A year later, he resigned as chairman of the White Star Line. Other than establishing funds for lost seamen and merchant marines, he kept a low public profile. He died in London in 1937 at age 74.

"When Will the Screaming Stop?"

Eva Hart

T he unearthly cries for help from those doomed to die reverberated in the frigid blackness, petrifying seven-year-old Eva Hart. In her packed lifeboat, the little girl screamed, trying to drown out the persistent moans and wails of hundreds upon hundreds of people who had jumped or been pitched off the sinking *Titanic* moments earlier.

The chilling drone of those unfortunate souls who were left bobbing in the deadly waters terrorized Eva to her core. No matter how loud she screeched or how hard she covered her ears, she could still hear the awful sounds of human misery. She thought, *When will the screaming stop?*

But with every unbearable minute that passed, the wretched noise slackened as, one by one, the freezing water stole the life of the ill-fated passengers.

Exhausted, Eva stopped crying. And then she heard

something that left her feeling even more afraid. Silence. Dead silence. To the shell-shocked girl, it was as if the whole world was standing still, paralyzed by the enormity of this unbelievable disaster. In the vast nothingness, even the stars—brighter than she ever had imagined—seemed to stop sparkling. Overwhelmed by the creepy quiet and stillness, she started screaming again.

Her mother, Esther, gave her a comforting hug, although what Eva wanted even more was feeling the strong arms of her father, Benjamin, and hearing his reassuring voice. But he wasn't in the lifeboat. He was somewhere out there in the dark, dying . . . or dead.

Just months earlier, Eva didn't have a care in the world, enjoying the love and warmth of her parents in Ilford, a village outside London, where Ben, 47, was a skilled carpenter and builder. Esther was 41 when she had Eva, their only child. The parents adored their willowy, raven-haired daughter—and she adored them.

During the Christmas holiday, a friend of her father's who had moved to Winnipeg, Manitoba, Canada, returned to Ilford for a visit. One evening, he had dinner at the Harts' home, where he talked about the prosperous life he had created in Winnipeg and encouraged Ben, who was having difficulty finding work, to join him. The next day, Ben announced that the family would move to Winnipeg to take advantage of the new opportunities that awaited them there.

"What about the risks?" Esther asked.

"I'll either sink or swim," he replied. It was an expression he used whenever he tried anything new.

Sitting Eva on his lap and calling her by her pet name, he said, "Baby, how would you like to live in a new country? We'll take a big boat across the ocean and then a train to a beautiful place where the sun shines almost every day and the trees remain green year-round and the lakes are sky blue."

"Oh, Daddy, that sounds like fun!"

As happy as her father was, Eva sensed her mother wasn't pleased by the move. For Esther, it meant leaving her friends and her elderly parents, and she worried that she would never see them again.

The Harts were booked on the ship *Philadelphia* to New York, where they planned to spend time with a relative of Ben's before taking a train across Canada to Winnipeg. But there was an unexpected change in their travel plans. Because of a strike by coal miners in the United Kingdom, there wasn't enough coal to fuel the *Philadelphia*. As a result, the Harts were given the opportunity to sail on the *Titanic*, whose owners had purchased enough coal for the crossing.

"Isn't this wonderful?" Ben told Eva and Esther. "We're going on the maiden voyage of the grandest ship ever built!"

Eva was thrilled because her father was so excited.

But she saw that her mother was aghast. "Isn't that the ship they say is unsinkable?" Esther asked.

"No," he replied, grinning. "That's the ship that *is* unsinkable."

"But, Ben, that's flying in the face of God," she claimed. "I am so frightened."

"Oh, don't be silly, Esther. We're fortunate to go on such a great vessel."

Eva could tell her mother wasn't convinced. "I dread the sea," Esther said. "The idea of being on the sea at night is bad enough for one night, but for six or seven, it will be a nightmare over and over for me."

"Nonsense," said Ben. "You'll love it."

Eva was awed by the vessel. The Harts had a cozy four-berth cabin in second class. Ben slept on the top berth of one bunk bed while Eva slept below with her doll and teddy bear. Esther took the lower berth on the other bunk. When they settled in, she said, "Well, I've made up my mind about one thing."

"What's that, Mummy?" Eva asked.

"Until we are safe in New York, I'm not going to sleep at night on this ship," she announced. "The crew will be less vigilant at night than during the day, so I'm going to be dressed and remain sitting up in bed throughout the night, fully prepared."

"Fully prepared for what?" Ben asked.

"For the worst, whatever that might be."

Eva seldom saw her parents argue, but in the cabin they quarreled over Esther's seemingly irrational fear. Their spat became so heated that for the first time in her life, Eva saw her mother cry. Nothing Ben said could persuade Esther to put aside her worries. True to her word, Esther stayed awake each night, lying in her bunk bed, fully dressed. In the morning, she'd join her family for breakfast and then sleep until 6 P.M., when she would have dinner with Eva and Ben.

Her mother's strange behavior didn't bother Eva. In fact, she was fine with it because it meant more one-on-one time with her father. With her long, curly tresses dancing in the breeze, she would race her dad back and forth on the Promenade Deck, play hide-and-seek, and shop. Ben always gave in to the urge to buy his precious daughter toys and trinkets that were sold, strangely, in the ship's barbershop.

Eva also enjoyed playing with a new friend she made on board, six-year-old Annie "Nina" Harper, of London. Nina was traveling with her widowed father, the Reverend John Harper, a Baptist minister, and her aunt, Jessie Leitch, to Chicago, where Harper was slated to conduct several tent revival meetings. Eva and Nina played with Eva's teddy bear and held pretend tea parties. They explored the ship, taking different passageways until they were stopped by ropes with signs that read, "No Second-Class Passengers Beyond This Point."

The day wasn't complete without frolicking with a friendly champion French bulldog named Gamin de Pycombe owned by first-class passenger Robert Daniel. After breakfast, Eva hurried to the ship's kennel, where she was allowed to walk the pooch, one of at least ten dogs on board. Most of the pets, though, were not kept in the kennels but in the cabins of their owners.

Seeing how much Eva loved the bulldog, Ben promised her, "Once we get settled in Winnipeg, I'll get you a dog of your own."

Eva threw her arms around his neck and squealed, "Oh, thank you, Daddy!"

On Saturday, Captain Edward Smith chatted with some of the second-class passengers, including Ben and Eva. His ruddy, round face and thick white beard reminded her of her grandfather. During the conversation, Eva told him, "Mummy is afraid something bad will happen to the ship."

Smith leaned down, patted Eva on the head, and said, "There's nothing to worry about because the *Titanic* is a wonderful, safe ship. Even God himself couldn't sink her."

That evening at dinner, Eva's mother admitted that although she was still troubled, she was feeling less anxious. "I'm about content as I can be at sea," she said.

That night while Eva and Ben were asleep, Esther, who remained dressed and alert in her lower bunk, suddenly let out a yelp that awakened Eva. Esther shook Ben and cried out, "Ben! Ben! Wake up! Something dreadful is happening!"

Clearing the fog from his brain, Ben sat up. "Huh? What's wrong?"

"I was resting, listening to the hum of the propellers, when I had this sensation that some gigantic force had given the ship a mighty push from behind not once, not twice, but three times. I was literally frozen in terror. I'm so frightened."

Ben groaned and plopped back on his pillow. "You're acting crazy, old girl. Your imagination is out of control. I'm going back to sleep."

"No! No! You must listen to me," she said, her voice breaking. "Ben, this is real. Please, you must see if we're in danger."

"Mummy, I'm getting scared," said sleepy-eyed Eva.

"Oh, I'm so sorry, Baby," said Esther, placing her trembling hand on Eva's shoulder. "Mummy needs Daddy to make sure everything is fine."

"You and your unfounded fears," muttered Ben as he threw a jacket over his pajamas. "I'll be back in a minute."

Moments later, he returned. "Everything is dandy," he said. "The sea is calm, the ship is traveling smoothly, and a crewman told me we're right on schedule. So you see, there's nothing to fuss about. Now, please, Esther, let us go back to sleep."

Whispering so Eva couldn't hear, Esther said, "What I felt was real. It's a warning of something bad, Ben. I just know it. If it hasn't happened yet, it's going to happen."

The next morning at breakfast, Ben laughingly told the family's dining companions about Esther's bizarre episode. "I have figured out what to do to keep her quiet tonight," he said with a chuckle. "I'm going to insist she drink a strong glass of hot grog to make her sleep, so she can't disrupt Eva's and my beauty rest."

Because it was Sunday, Esther joined Eva and Ben for church services in the lounge and then ate lunch with them for the first time. That evening, Eva and her father were sleeping when once again, Esther shook Ben awake. "Ben, get up at once! We have hit something. I am sure of it, and it's serious."

"Oh, woman, not again," he growled. "I'm at my wit's end. I don't know what to do with you."

"Ben, this is real and it's happening right now. I just heard the most awful sound I have ever heard in my life—a dreadful tearing and ripping sound. It was the sound of great masses of steel being violently torn."

"Mummy, what's wrong?" mumbled Eva, opening her eyes.

"Baby, Daddy needs to find out something." Glaring at Ben, Esther said, "I insist you investigate right now."

None too pleased, Ben grumbled under his breath as he threw on his coat over his pajamas and stormed out of the cabin in his bare feet.

"Come, Baby, let's get you dressed," Esther said to Eva.

"No, Mummy, I want to go back to sleep." Eva rolled over and covered her head with the blanket.

While Esther rousted Eva out of bed, Ben returned. Eva noticed he had the same scared look that her mother displayed moments earlier.

"I don't have to ask you what happened," Esther told him. "I know it's bad."

"We need to get on the Boat Deck right away."

Ben quickly donned pants over his pajamas and put on his shoes and an overcoat. After Eva was dressed, he wrapped her in a blanket and draped his heavy sheepskin-lined coat over Esther's shoulders. Then he led them to the upper deck.

On the way, they met a stewardess who told them, "Everything is all right. It's only a lifeboat drill."

"Don't be silly," Esther scoffed, brushing her aside. "They don't have lifeboat drills at midnight."

The Harts arrived on the Boat Deck, which was bustling with activity. Word had spread that the ship had struck an iceberg. Now fully awake, Eva was getting scared, especially when she saw her father off to the side, quietly praying.

As the deck grew more crowded with passengers and crew, Eva heard someone yell, "She can't stay afloat!"

Holding hands, the Harts hurried from one lifeboat station to another, only to be told they were already full. After failing to gain access in the first four boats they tried, they found room in Lifeboat 14. Ben handed Eva to a crewman in the boat and then helped Esther in. "Hold Mummy's hand and be a good girl," Ben told Eva.

When a teenage boy was ordered out of the boat, Fifth Officer Harold Lowe pulled out his revolver and threatened to shoot him. Then other men surged forward. "Stand back!" Lowe ordered. "I say, stand back! The next man who puts his foot in this boat, I will shoot him down like a dog." He pointed the gun at Ben, who was assisting other women and children into the boat. His foot was already in the boat.

"Don't shoot my daddy," Eva pleaded. "Please, don't shoot my daddy."

Ben told Lowe, "I'm not going in. But for God's sake, look after my wife and child."

Moments later, the lifeboat, with Lowe and three crewmen on board, was lowered. As it rowed away from the stricken *Titanic*, most of the women and children were sobbing. Lowe, who was standing at the stern, tried to quiet them. "Don't cry," he urged. "Please don't cry. I'll give you something else to do than cry. Some can start bailing water. Others help handle the oars. But, please, stop crying."

Eva tried to stifle her sobbing, but she couldn't. She was terrified.

"Help Mummy bail," Esther told her.

As they used a bailer to get the water out, Eva said, "I keep kicking something soft under my seat."

Esther reached down and felt around until she touched a cold, shivering person. "My word!" she yelled. "There's a poor wretch hiding under me!"

Esther, Eva, and several other women shifted positions as a slender, small man in a woman's coat emerged. When he came out, he was so stiff he could scarcely move. Efforts to get him to talk failed because he didn't speak English. Apparently, the stowaway had sneaked into the boat before it was loaded and had hid under the seat in about six inches of freezing water.

"He might be a coward but he's a human being," said Esther. "Let's try to keep him alive." She and several women next to her rubbed his arms and legs to bring back his circulation.

Meanwhile, Eva was crying herself sick, vomiting several times. She wailed the loudest while watching the *Titanic* break apart and sink. When the water closed over the vessel, the once smooth surface heaved with the unlucky people who were destined to die. Many in their life vests begged for rescue; others flailed helplessly among floating debris, including chairs, pillows, rugs, benches, tables, and food.

Lowe insisted on going back to pick up anyone still alive in the water. But to make room for possible survivors, he had to transfer many people from his lifeboat to others that were less crowded. A crewman picked up Eva and put her in the arms of a woman in another lifeboat on the starboard side. The little girl expected that her mother would follow her. But in the confusion, Esther ended up in a boat on the port side after nearly falling into the water during the transfer.

"Mummy!" Eva shrieked. "I want my mummy!"

"I'm close by, Baby!" her mother hollered in the darkness. "Be brave!"

Eva couldn't. She kept howling and vomiting until she quieted down from sheer exhaustion, much to the relief of the passengers in her boat.

When the sun finally peeked over the horizon, Eva thought she was dreaming, because it looked as if her lifeboat was floating among an enormous fleet of yachts with glistening sails spread full. She then realized they were really sparkling icebergs, moving slowly and majestically in the water that had turned choppy at daybreak.

Maneuvering among the icebergs, the steamer

Carpathia began picking up the survivors, one lifeboat at a time. Eva was hauled up in a boatswain's chair. When she finally reached the deck of the rescue ship, the little girl searched among the hundreds of dazed, weeping women who were grieving over their lost loved ones.

After what seemed like hours for Eva, but was really only minutes, she finally nestled into the comforting and tearful embrace of her mother. "Where's Daddy?" Eva asked.

Choking back sobs, Esther said, "I don't know, Baby. It might be a long time before we find out where he is." Esther couldn't bring herself to tell Eva that her father was never coming back.

Eva's friend Nina couldn't understand why her father, too, wasn't on board the *Carpathia*. When the *Titanic* began sinking, Rev. Harper had wrapped Nina in a blanket, kissed her good-bye, and handed her to a crewman, who put her into Lifeboat 11 with her aunt, Jessie Leitch. Now Rev. Harper was among the missing.

"I left Papa on the big boat, and he told me to go with Aunt Jessie," she told Eva. "Now I want Papa."

Two days later, as the *Carpathia* steamed toward New York, Eva overheard her mother talking to several women who had lost their husbands. ". . . So that was the last I saw of my poor lost dear husband," Esther said in a quavering voice. "No farewell kiss, no fond words. In a moment he was gone. I knew that I had seen the last of my Ben, and that I had lost the best and truest friend, the kindest and most thoughtful husband that a woman ever had."

Esther started to cry. When she regained her composure, she talked about the emotional trauma Eva would face. "What an experience for a little child to go through—at the age of seven to have passed through the valley of the shadow of death. I wonder if she will ever forget it. I know I won't if I live for a hundred years."

Benjamin Hart's body was never found. Neither was Rev. John Harper's.

After a short stay in New York, Eva and her mother returned to England, as did Nina and her aunt. Orphaned at the age of six, Nina was raised by relatives and later married a minister. She died at the age of 80 in 1986.

Eva and her mother lived with Esther's parents near London until Esther remarried. Throughout the rest of her childhood and into her twenties, Eva was plagued with nightmares stemming from the Titanic tragedy. She also feared any large body of water.

"I would wake up in a terrible panic, and then I would rush into my mother's room and she would comfort me," Eva said in a 1993 interview with the BBC. "But when she died, I didn't have her around anymore." A few months after her mother's death, Eva, who was then

23, felt the only way to overcome the nightmares and conquer her fear was to go to sea, so she booked passage to Singapore.

"The first four days at sea I wouldn't come out of my cabin," she recalled. "I kept telling the stewardess that I was seasick. She knew it wasn't true. I was too frightened. She made me get up on deck, and from then on, I lost that terror. Although I don't like the sea, I had no more nightmares. But I still can remember the colors, the sounds, everything from that night. The worst thing I remember are the screams and then the silence that followed."

Later in life, Eva became an outspoken Titanic survivor. She repeatedly criticized the White Star Line for failing to provide enough lifeboats. She also condemned salvagers for their "insensitivity and greed" when they began bringing up artifacts from the wreck in 1987. She said the site was the resting place of nearly fifteen hundred people, including her father, and "should be left as a grave for those who never should have died."

Eva, who never married, was a professional singer as well as a music teacher. During World War II, she entertained the troops and distributed emergency supplies in London after bombing raids. A volunteer for numerous charities, she became a justice of the peace later in life. She died in 1996 at her home outside London. Eva Hart was 91.

"Father Is Never Coming Home"

John "Jack" Ryerson

Thirteen-year-old John "Jack" Ryerson was looking forward to another fantastic day in Paris with his family when the tragic news struck like a crackling thunderbolt: His big brother, Arthur Jr., a 20-year-old Yale student, had been killed in a car crash outside of Philadelphia.

Jack suffered the same shock and disbelief as his parents, retired millionaire attorney Arthur Ryerson Sr., and Emily Ryerson; and his sisters, Susan, 21, and Emily, 18. (Another sister, Ellen, was at a boarding school in Maryland.)

Up until that awful morning, the day after Easter, April 8, 1912, the Ryersons had been enjoying a marvelous vacation. In February, they had closed up their mansion in Haverford, Pennsylvania, and left on an extended tour of Europe. Traveling with them were Jack's tutor, Grace Bowen, and Mrs. Ryerson's personal French maid, Victorine Chaudanson, who also was helping the girls brush up on their French. One of the reasons for the trip was for Susan and Emily to meet some of Europe's eligible—and preferably wealthy—bachelors and size them up as possible future husbands.

The Ryersons were staying at the elegant Hotel Langham in Paris when the cable arrived informing them of Arthur Jr.'s death. He had been riding in an open car driven by his pal John Hoffman—who was also a Yale student born into a rich, prominent family—in the countryside. Unexpectedly, John lost control of the car. It careened into a ditch and slammed into a telegraph pole, hurling both young men over the hood. John's head struck the pole while Arthur was thrown against a fence post. Both died later that evening.

As they coped with their grief, Jack's parents made plans to return home on the first available ship leaving for New York. That would be the *Titanic*. They booked first-class passage on the vessel, which was scheduled to arrive on Wednesday, April 17. The funeral service was slated for Friday at St. Mark's Episcopal Church in Philadelphia, with burial in the family plot overlooking Otsego Lake, near their summer estate, Ringwood, outside of Cooperstown, New York.

Jack was shrouded in a mental fog. He couldn't

believe that his big brother was dead. The boy always looked up to him and relished his visits home from college. It was hard for Jack to fathom there would be no more golf lessons from Arthur, no more wrestling each other out on the lawn, no more playing doubles together on the tennis court.

At the hotel, Jack gathered up his books and schoolwork for the trip home. Miss Bowen and Victorine hastily packed the family's clothing, personal items, and their bed linens. The next morning, 16 steamer trunks were ready for transport. Everyone in the group was dressed in somber mourning clothes, with Jack and his father each wearing a black armband. They boarded the Train Transatlantique for the six-hour trip to Cherbourg, France, the first of two stops by the *Titanic*.

On the train, the Ryersons met by chance several socially prominent friends who had booked passage on the *Titanic* after wintering in Europe. Among them were Colonel John Jacob Astor IV and his new teen-age wife, Madeleine, and wealthy Philadelphians John and Marian Thayer and George and Eleanor "Nellie" Widener. The friends were stunned and saddened to learn of Arthur Jr.'s death.

The following evening, the group stepped aboard the tender *Nomadic*, which ferried them out to the great ship anchored in the Cherbourg harbor. The

Titanic, in all its majesty, awed Jack, offering him a momentary respite from his sorrow. Set against a spectacular purple and gold sunset, the towering vessel sparkled with thousands of lights from bow to stern.

Once on board, the Ryersons were greeted by J. Bruce Ismay, head of the White Star Line. After extending his condolences, he gave them their own personal steward and another stateroom in addition to the two they had already booked. Their suites on the starboard side of B Deck provided them with three bedrooms, two bathrooms, and four large walk-in closets. Jack shared a room with Emily; Miss Bowen stayed with Susan; and Mr. and Mrs. Ryerson had their own suite. Victorine was given a room down the hall.

Jack spent the next few days exploring the ship and using the gymnasium, which was open to children every afternoon from 1 to 3 P.M. As a diversion from their grief, he and his sisters sometimes played shuffleboard or quoits (a ring-toss game).

Jack worried about his mother, who remained in deep mourning and rarely left her stateroom. At mealtimes, while the rest of the family ate in the dining saloon, Mrs. Ryerson stayed in her suite, nibbling at food the steward brought to her on a silver tray.

"Mother, please, won't you come with me and see

this grand ship?" Jack asked. "It has so many splendid things."

"Jack, it's better if I stay put," she replied. "I know many people on this ship, and I really don't want to see any of them just now. They will be very sympathetic and then they will engage in small talk. I just couldn't bear that. It wouldn't be proper."

He was relieved that his father had at least convinced her to go for nightly walks. Wearing a black veil around her feathered hat, Mrs. Ryerson would hook her arm around her husband's and go for a long stroll every night when the decks were nearly deserted.

On Sunday morning, Jack, his sisters, and his father attended a church service held in the first-class dining saloon. The boy choked up when he saw his father, a man of strong faith, moved to tears during the singing of the hymn "O God, Our Help in Ages Past."

That night, Jack and Emily were sound asleep when their mother pounded on the door and shouted, "Emily! Jack! Wake up! Get dressed immediately!" Mrs. Ryerson then roused Susan and Miss Bowen from bed before running down the hall to wake up Victorine.

Jack quickly dressed, but Emily was still so sleepy she could barely get out of bed. When their mother returned, she scolded Emily. "You're so slow! Don't bother putting on a dress. There's not enough time. Just put on your fur coat right over your nightgown like I've done. And bring your life jacket. Hurry!"

"Mother, what's the matter?" Jack asked.

"There's talk that we've struck an iceberg. Captain Smith has ordered all passengers to report to the Boat Deck right away."

When the Ryerson group gathered in the hallway, Mr. Ryerson checked the straps on all their life jackets. Then he led them down the corridor to the Grand Staircase and up to the port side of the Boat Deck, where they were joined by the Thayers, Wideners, Astors, and William and Lucile Carter and their two children, Billy and Lucile. They were assigned to Lifeboat 4. But it wasn't ready because of unexpected delays.

The deck was listing to port and the bow was sinking by the minute. While other lifeboats carrying women and children were being lowered into the water, the group stood around in the cold, assaulted by the noise of the roaring steam vents. These rich and powerful people had been used to giving orders their whole lives, but on this night they patiently waited for instructions on where to go.

While they worried, Jack was enthralled by the flares being fired into the sky to attract any ships that might be in the area. The flares reminded him of the fireworks on the Fourth of July over Otsego Lake.

Colonel Astor tried to assure everyone that there

was little danger. "Even if, for some unimaginable reason, the *Titanic* can't stay afloat," he said, "I have been informed that the *Olympic* and the *Baltic* are on the way to give assistance. They will remove those of us who don't get into lifeboats."

Finally, at about 1:30 A.M., the group was ordered down to the Promenade Deck where the loading of No. 4 began—the wealthy women and their maids, mothers from third class clutching their babies, women and children from Lebanon and Sweden. Wives kissed their husbands and stepped into the boat.

Eventually, it was the Ryersons' turn. But Jack's mother balked. "Why must I go in that boat?" she asked her husband. "Please, let me stay with you."

"Now, Emily," he replied. "You must follow orders. I'll remain with John Thayer. We'll be all right."

"Let the others go first," she said.

Jack's father helped Miss Bowen into the boat. Then he kissed and hugged his two daughters before assisting Victorine.

"Please take my place in the boat, Mr. Ryerson," the maid said. "If I died, who would mourn?"

"Thank you, Victorine, but you're not going to die, and I will not take your place in the boat." He then handed her off to Second Officer Charles Lightoller, who was in charge of the loading.

Next in line was Jack, who was standing in front of

his mother. Jack hugged his father and then started to climb into the boat when Lightoller declared, "He can't go. Women and children only."

Jack's father grabbed Lightoller by the arm and turned him so they were nose to nose. Speaking from the deep anguish of a father who had just lost a son and wasn't about to risk losing another one, Mr. Ryerson asserted, "Of course that boy goes with his mother. He's only thirteen years old!"

Intimidated by Mr. Ryerson's intensity, the officer nodded and let Jack climb in. Trying to regain his authority, Lightoller announced, "No more boys!"

From his seat next to Miss Bowen in the stern, Jack watched his parents embrace and kiss each other before his mother entered No. 4. In her haste, she fell awkwardly over several other women who were already in the boat. Regaining her balance, she scrambled to a seat in the bow beside Susan. Victorine and Emily had taken their places in the middle of the boat near Marian Thayer and Madeleine Astor. It was almost 2 A.M.

Even though the boat was only half full, Lightoller ordered it lowered. Jack and his sisters waved to their father, who was standing by the railing with Thayer, Astor, and Widener. Mr. Ryerson waved back and smiled.

Jack noticed how far the ship had already sunk. The deck used to be 60 feet above the waterline but was now less than 20 feet from the surface. He saw water rushing in through open portholes of the deluxe suites on B and C Decks. He watched deck chairs, doors, and casks being hurled off the decks from above—objects meant for people to cling to after they jumped or fell into the water.

There were only two seamen in the lifeboat, so Marian Thayer, Madeleine Astor, Lucile Carter, and other women in the middle pulled on the oars. As No. 4 moved away from the ship, quartermaster Walter Perkis, who was in charge of the lifeboat, yelled, "She's going! Pull for your lives, or we'll be sucked under!" Everyone who was by an oar—including Emily and Victorine—rowed with all the strength they could muster.

Within a few cruel minutes the *Titanic* was no more.

Suddenly, the black water was teeming with drowning, freezing people shrieking for help. "We need to go back and save those poor souls!" Mrs. Ryerson shouted.

"No," countered others in the lifeboat. "They'll capsize us!"

"We absolutely must," Mrs. Ryerson insisted. "Our husbands could be dying out there."

Perkis ordered No. 4 to turn around, and they began hauling waterlogged, freezing men aboard. Some were barely conscious. As each man was pulled in, the women rubbed his numb, ice-cold arms and legs to increase circulation.

Jack kept wondering if the next person they saved would be his father . . . or the next . . . or the next. The boy figured that if his father hadn't made it into a lifeboat, he was probably still alive because he was a strong swimmer. For a 61-year-old, Mr. Ryerson was extremely fit. But after a dozen men — all crewmembers — were rescued, no more survivors were found. The anxiety over his father's fate heightened when two of the men they had plucked out of the icy water died within the first hour. Jack knew then that without a lifeboat, there was no hope.

Seeing how downcast he was, Miss Bowen tried to interest him in the sky. "Oh, Jack, have you ever seen so many beautiful stars?" she asked. "They seem so big and bright, it's almost as though you could reach out and touch them. Look, there's the Big Dipper. And over there. See those three bright stars in a row? They form Orion's Belt." She kept pointing out different constellations and telling him the legends behind the names.

Jack and the others suffered through the brutally cold night in a daze, dumbfounded by the tragedy. Their spirits soared, however, when the rescue ship *Carpathia* came into view at dawn. It took another two hours before they were brought aboard. When Jack stepped foot on the deck, he was given hot chocolate. Never had a drink tasted so good to him. Wrapped in warm blankets, he and his sisters began to thaw out.

But his mother remained in her frost-covered fur coat, her hands gripping the railing, her eyes scanning each arriving lifeboat for her husband.

Jack and his sisters watched, too. When the last man from the last lifeboat came aboard, Mrs. Ryerson nearly collapsed. Emotionally drained and exhausted, she was led from the railing by her children. Slumped in a chair, she refused to accept that her husband was dead. "He must have been picked up by another ship," she told her children. "He's still alive. I just know it."

Jack desperately wanted to believe her. He had already lost a brother; he didn't want to lose a father, too.

After a short memorial service over the spot where the *Titanic* went down, the *Carpathia* steamed for New York. During the four-day trip, the ship endured fog, thunderstorms, and heavy seas, which only added to the misery of the survivors—hundreds of whom were now widowed.

Despite her grief, Mrs. Ryerson felt the pain and suffering of those survivors who lost everything but their lives. So she, Mrs. Widener, Mrs. Thayer, and Mrs. Astor, who had all lost their husbands, agreed to set up a special fund for penniless survivors. The wealthy women promised to make their contributions once they landed in New York.

By the time the *Carpathia* docked Thursday night, Jack had accepted his father's death. Waiting for the Ryersons was his youngest sister, Ellen, who had brought extra coats and wraps for everyone. When she saw her brother, she rushed up and hugged him. "You're alive!" she squealed. "The newspaper this morning counted you and Father among the dead. Does this mean he's alive, too?"

Jack shook his head glumly and said, "Father is never coming home."

Holding his mother's hand, Jack walked with her and his sisters to a waiting limousine, which whisked them to the Hotel Belmont. A personal shopper for the family then bought each of them proper mourning clothes, which were delivered to the hotel. On Sunday morning, the Ryersons attended St. Thomas Church, where the Reverend Ernest Stires paid tribute to Colonel Astor and Arthur Ryerson Sr.

Later that week, the family accompanied the body of Arthur Jr. to Cooperstown for burial. The casket containing Arthur Jr.'s body rested on a bank of greens and flowers on a farm wagon from Ringwood and was drawn by a pair of horses. The long line of carriages bearing mourners and family friends passed through the small town. On Main Street, the curtains of the storefronts were drawn and flags were at half-staff in sympathy of the Ryersons. The vested choir of Christ

Church sang "Alleluia" while the body was being lowered into the grave at Lakewood Cemetery.

Jack, his sisters, and mother had finally carried out the heart-rending mission that had caused them to take the ill-fated *Titanic*.

Arthur Ryerson Sr.'s body was never recovered.

Two years after the Titanic tragedy, Jack and his mother went on an eight-month trip around the world. After graduating from Yale, Jack made golf his passion. He played in 425 amateur tournaments throughout the 1930s and 1940s, and eventually golfed on more than 1,400 different courses. In the early 1960s, he deeded the Ringwood estate of 28 rooms and 37 acres to the Episcopal Church to use as a youth center. He waited until he was 54 before he married and settled in Palm Beach, Florida, where he died at age 87 in 1986. He seldom talked about the Titanic. Jack is buried in the Ryerson family plot in Lakewood Cemetery.

To ease her grief over the death of her husband, Mrs. Emily Ryerson threw herself into charity work. During World War I, she raised money for wounded French soldiers and fatherless children, and was awarded one of France's highest honors, the Croix de Guerre. As a tribute to Arthur Jr., she endowed a Yale scholarship in his name to be awarded annually to a student "who exhibits good character and exceptional promise." She traveled on goodwill trips on behalf of President Herbert Hoover and helped raise money for the European Children's Relief Fund. In 1927, she married Forsythe Sherfesee, a financial advisor to the Chinese government. The couple, who had a villa on the French Riviera, traveled the world. Emily Ryerson Sherfesee died of a heart attack at age 76 in Uruguay in 1939. She is buried in the Ryerson family plot.

Jack's sister Susan, who had attended the University of Chicago, worked at an army field hospital in France during World War I. For weeks while transporting the wounded in her ambulance, she was under constant enemy fire. Like her mother, Susan was awarded the Croix de Guerre. She married Lieutenant George Patterson, an American war hero who was also a recipient of the medal, and moved to Morristown, New Jersey. Tragically, Susan died in 1921 at age 30 from complications caused by appendicitis. She is buried in the Ryerson family plot.

Jack's sister Emily was married twice and had seven children. She lived at Ringwood until her death in 1960 at age 66. She is buried in the Ryerson family plot. In a tragic twist of fate, her grandson, Christopher Coulson, was a student at Yale who was killed in a car accident while home on a holiday vacation—just like Arthur Jr.

Two months after the Titanic disaster, the Ryersons' maid, Victorine Chaudanson, married the family's chauffeur, Henry Perkins. They spent most of their lives in New York. She died in 1962 at age 86.

Jack's tutor, Grace Bowen, devoted the rest of her life to teaching in the Cooperstown area. She was 78 when she died in 1945.

(Some of the source material for this story came from an article written by Phyllis Ryerse, which was published in the summer 1990 issue of the Titanic Historical Society's The Titanic Commutator.)

"They're Leaving Without Me!"

Ruth Becker

In the growing confusion and chaos of the sinking
Titanic, 12-year-old Ruth Becker stood rooted to the
slanting deck and stared at her anguished mother, who
had just been tossed into crowded Lifeboat 11 along
with Ruth's younger sister and baby brother.

"Find another boat, Ruth!" her mother pleaded as
the boat was being lowered.

"Hurry and find another boat!"

From the railing Ruth watched the lifeboat descend
and could still hear her mother's tormented cries. The
girl was now totally on her own.

All but two of the sixteen wooden lifeboats had
already been launched . . . and time was slipping away
before the vessel would sink to the bottom. On a deck
teeming with hundreds upon hundreds of terrified passengers who were shoving and elbowing each other,
Ruth needed to get into one of the remaining lifeboats.

Unlike most who didn't know where to go or what to do, Ruth didn't panic. Her gentle manner and sweet face belied her maturity and mettle. As the daughter of missionaries in India, she had seen more danger and death than most adults saw in a lifetime. For much of her childhood, Ruth had lived in a modest home amid India's squalor and poverty. She had encountered monsoons and typhoons. At a young age, she had learned to think for herself and believe in herself. And to have faith.

Although she was American, Ruth was born in Guntur, India, where her father, Reverend Allen Becker, a Lutheran minister, and her mother, Nellie, worked as missionaries. Her 4-year-old sister, Marion, and 21-month-old brother Richard were also born in that country. Ruth had another brother, Luther, who died in 1907 from an illness when he was two and she was eight.

Early in 1912, Richard contracted an illness similar to the one that had taken Luther's life. Fearing that if the boy stayed in India he would suffer the same fate as his brother, the Beckers decided to move to Benton Harbor, Michigan, where medical care was much better.

Ruth's father was also in poor health, but there wasn't enough time for him to get the necessary authorization for a medical leave. "I will come later," he told Ruth. Seeing tears welling up in her eyes, he handed her one of his handkerchiefs. "Keep it," he said. "You can give it back to me when I return home."

After packing up much of their belongings, Ruth, her siblings, and her mother traveled to the city of Madras (now called Chennai), where they boarded a steamer on March 7, 1912. During the month-long trip, they sailed across the Indian Ocean, through the Suez Canal, across the Mediterranean Sea, up the coasts of Portugal, Spain, and France, and finally to London, England, arriving on April 5. Over the next five days, Nellie took the kids to see Westminster Abbey, Madame Tussaud's Wax Museum, St. Paul's Cathedral, and the London Zoo.

Early Wednesday morning, April 10, the family took the boat train that carried second- and third-class passengers to the docks of Southampton. They boarded the *Titanic* about 10:30 A.M.

Having just spent a month on a steamer, Ruth wasn't thrilled about getting on another ship. But when she cast her eyes on the *Titanic* for the first time, she was impressed with its grandeur. She was even more in awe when they stepped into their second-class cabin, 4-F, which was on the port side toward the stern and close to the waterline.

During the voyage, Nellie usually watched over Marion, while Ruth spent her time with Richard. Ruth often took him to the enclosed Promenade Deck, where she wheeled him from one end to the other in a stroller provided by the White Star Line.

Shortly after midnight on Sunday night, Ruth and her mother were awakened by people running up the stairs and loud voices in the hallway.

"The ship has stopped," said Ruth, sitting up in bed. "What do you think is going on?"

"I'll find out," Nellie replied. She put a robe over her nightclothes and left the cabin. Minutes later she returned. "I talked to a steward. He said there's been a little accident and they're fixing it, and then we'll be on our way."

"Oh, okay," said Ruth. She lay her head on her pillow to go back to sleep, but she couldn't close her eyes. Neither could her mother. Both were getting concerned by the constant footsteps pounding up and down the passageway and by the urgent tone of the voices outside. Adding to the anxiety, the engines hadn't started up.

Nellie hopped out of bed and told Ruth, "I'm going to find another steward and get to the bottom of this."

Shortly after she left, Nellie burst into the room and announced, "Get the little ones up at once and help me get them dressed. Hurry!"

"What's wrong, Mama?"

"A steward just told me to put on our life vests and go up to the A Deck immediately. The ship is in trouble."

Ruth awakened Richard, who was cranky from getting up. As she dressed him, he began to cry and so did Marion, who was being helped into her clothes by Nellie. Ruth and Nellie were in such a rush that they didn't even bother to dress themselves. They just threw their coats on over their nightclothes, picked up the children, and dashed out of the cabin. They didn't even take time to put on their life jackets.

They ran up the steps and into the lounge, which was filling up with women and children in various states of dress. Some were crying and whimpering; others were trying to comfort them. Soon two officers entered the lounge and announced, "It's time for all the women and children to get into the lifeboats."

One of the officers took Richard from Ruth's arms while the other carried Marion and said, "Follow us." They climbed an iron ladder to the Boat Deck, where crewmen were preparing to launch the lifeboats.

Out in the open in the freezing night air, Nellie and the children began to shiver. "It's so very cold," Nellie said. "Ruth, honey, run back to our cabin and get blankets for us. And please hurry!"

Weaving her way against the current of passengers who were streaming out of the lower decks, Ruth hustled into the cabin, grabbed the blankets off each of the beds, and scampered back on deck. By now, the deck was much more crowded and she had to squirm and squeeze her way through the pack.

As she neared the station for Lifeboat 11, she saw crewmen hand Richard and Marion over to women in the boat. "That's all for this boat!" an officer yelled. "Go ahead and lower it!"

Nellie, who was still standing on the deck, screamed, "Please, let me in! Those are my children, my babies!"

The officer grabbed Nellie by the hand and yanked her into the lifeboat, which now dangled over the side. "Lower away!"

Clutching the blankets to her chest, Ruth rushed up to the boat as it began its descent. *They're leaving without me!* "Mama?"

"Oh, dear lord!" Nellie cried, flinging her arms out in a sign of helplessness. "Ruth, honey, find another boat! Hurry!"

Ruth stared into the anguished eyes of her mother as Lifeboat 11 was jerkily winched down toward the inky water. The girl didn't flinch; she didn't cry. She knew — she just *knew* — that somehow she would survive. Ruth scampered to the next station, Lifeboat 13, which was crammed with more than 60 people. "Can I get in that boat?" she asked the officer in charge.

"We'll make room," he answered. Then he picked her up and tossed her into the boat. She landed in a heap among the passengers, which included some men who were allowed to board when the officer didn't see any more women or children in the area. Also in the boat were ten members of the crew, including five stokers—men who tended to the ship's coal-burning boilers. By the time she untangled herself, No. 13 was being lowered.

The pulley blocks creaked and groaned from the strain of the falls going through them. The crewmen aboard the lifeboat kept shouting up to their comrades on top to "keep the boat level."

The lifeboat was about ten feet from the surface directly above the exhaust from the *Titanic*'s condensers, which was spewing a huge stream of water from the ship's side just above the waterline. After the lifeboat reached the water, the stream from the exhaust shoved the boat—which was still attached by falls to the davits on the upper deck—toward the stern of the ship.

Lifeboat 13 was now directly under descending Lifeboat 15. Ruth looked up and gulped. No. 15 was 20 feet above her boat, and unless something was done immediately, it would smash on top of No. 13.

"Stop lowering fifteen!" the stokers shouted from No. 13. But the crew on board the ship couldn't hear them and kept lowering No. 15, which was now so close that several men in No. 13 stood and reached up, futilely trying to push aside the swaying hull of No. 15. Ruth cowered, knowing the next drop would land No. 15

right on their heads and either crush them or cause their boat to capsize.

Stokers on No. 13 whipped out their knives and frantically cut the falls. With only seconds to spare, No. 13 was freed and was pushed clear of No. 15 by the condensers' exhaust stream.

As the crewmen got the oars out, one of the stokers was grimacing in pain. In the frantic rush to cut the falls, he accidentally slashed his index finger to the bone and couldn't stem the bleeding. Ruth, who was nearby, reached into her coat pocket and pulled out her father's handkerchief. Even though it was a keepsake, she felt her father wouldn't mind putting it to good use. "Here, let me help you," she told the stoker. Then she wrapped the hanky around his severely injured finger.

While rowing away from the *Titanic*, the crewmen chose stoker Fred Barrett to be their "captain" and agreed to obey his orders. He called out to the other lifeboats and then ordered his rowers to head toward them. "When the rescue ship comes in the morning to look for us, we'll have a better chance of being found by keeping together," he said.

Ruth felt sad for the people lining the railings and watching the last lifeboats pull away. She wondered what they were thinking as they awaited almost certain death. *Are they wishing someone would come rescue them? Are they making their peace with God?*

Are they feeling angry or are they giving up?

Unlike most of the people in the lifeboat, Ruth wasn't scared. She had her faith and strong, positive thoughts. The spectacular starry night and the remarkably peaceful ocean provided her with a sense of serenity.

"I've been at sea twenty-six years, and I've never seen such a calm night on the Atlantic," Barrett told his passengers.

The ocean was so smooth and the night so still, it reminded Ruth of floating aimlessly in a rowboat on a mill pond on a summer's eve. She tried to keep that picture in her mind to help her ignore the awful cold.

Still clutching the four blankets she had retrieved from her cabin, Ruth realized that the stokers were in sleeveless shirts and shorts. She handed the blankets to the crewmen, who cut them in half and passed them out to those who had no protection from the freezing temperatures.

One young woman had been sobbing from the moment she got into No. 13. She was sitting next to Ruth, who tried to console her but wasn't having much success. Ruth had a hard time understanding her at first because the woman, 18-year-old Leah Aks, was distraught and had a thick Polish accent.

After Ruth calmed her down, Leah tearfully explained that she was missing her ten-month-old son, Frank Philip, whom she called Filly. She had booked third-class passage on the *Titanic* to reunite with her husband, Samuel, a tailor who had gone to Norfolk, Virginia, earlier to establish himself before sending for his family.

Leah said that when she was told to abandon ship, she wrapped Filly in a blanket and, with the help of several kind crewmen, made it to the Boat Deck. "The passengers were pushing and shoving to get into the lifeboats, and in the crush, my baby was knocked from my arms," she told Ruth. "It happened so quickly that I didn't see where my baby went. I asked everybody to help me find him, and everybody looked but they couldn't find Filly." She buried her head in her hands and wept. "He must have been kicked overboard in all the rush. My poor little Filly is dead."

"You don't know that," said Ruth. "There's good reason to hope otherwise. You probably couldn't find your baby because someone had picked him up and put him in a lifeboat."

"If only that were true."

Ruth put her arm around her and said, "When the rescue boat comes and picks us up, I'll help you find him."

Ruth felt confident that she would also reunite with her mother, Richard, and Marion. Everyone just needed to make it through the teeth-chattering night. She had given up the blankets, so all she had to keep warm was the coat over her nightclothes—and that wasn't doing the job. Every bone in her body ached from the cold. It hurt to move her frozen joints.

Off and on, Leah sobbed. During one outburst, she wailed, "I've lost everything! My precious Filly and all I owned. I have no money. Samuel sent me all the money he had for me to buy passage to America. And now we must start over . . . if that's even possible. Oh, Filly . . ."

"You must keep believing that Filly is alive," Ruth stressed. "Have faith."

Ruth kept peering into the darkness, searching for the first sign of lights from the rescue ship. Shortly before dawn, Barrett shouted, "I see two lights above the horizon! It's the *Carpathia*! Swing the boat toward her and row hard." As No. 13 headed toward the ship, Barrett bellowed, "Let's sing, boys!" The stokers broke out into a loud and happy rendition of the maritime tune "Row to the Shore, Sailors."

Ruth hugged Leah and said, "Isn't this great? We'll be on board in no time and then we'll find your baby."

"Oh, I hope you're right, but what if he's not there? What if . . ."

"Don't think like that. He *has* to be in one of the lifeboats."

When it was No. 13's turn to row up to the *Carpathia* and unload, crewmembers from the ship lowered a boatswain's chair so they could hoist Ruth and those who couldn't climb the Jacob's ladder. She sat in the chair but her fingers were so numb that she couldn't hold on to the ropes. Barrett had to tie her hands to the ropes before she was pulled up to the deck.

An officer who was greeting each survivor as he or she was brought aboard handed Ruth a blanket and said, "Would you like some hot coffee and brandy to warm you up?"

As cold as she was, Ruth declined. She had never tasted either drink and didn't think her stomach could handle it. After getting her numb feet and legs to move properly, Ruth went with Leah in search of Filly. Survivors who had arrived earlier from other lifeboats were scattered in different parts of the ship. Most were still in a daze or overcome with emotion. Some were being treated by one of the three doctors on board or were consuming warm food and drinks. Others had already fallen asleep in lounges and dining rooms or in cabins that sympathetic passengers shared with them.

"What was Filly wearing?" Ruth asked Leah.

"He was in blue nightwear and a scarf," she replied. "I remember that when Filly and I went on deck this nice woman of means took off her white silk scarf and wrapped it around his head."

They stopped people and asked if they knew of anyone with an infant. What few babies Ruth and Leah saw were not Filly. Leah was getting more frantic with each passing hour. There was still no word, no sign that Filly had been rescued. While helping Leah, Ruth also was looking for her own family. Shortly after the survivors from all the lifeboats had been brought on board, an acquaintance Ruth had met on the *Titanic* came up to her and said, "You're Ruth Becker, right?"

"Yes."

"Your mother has been searching everywhere for you. I'll take you to her."

"Oh, thank heaven!" Turning to Leah, Ruth said, "I must see my family." She left Leah, who was all but convinced that her baby had perished. Minutes later Nellie was smothering Ruth in hugs and kisses.

"I was so afraid you didn't make it into one of the other lifeboats," Nellie said, refusing to let go of Ruth. "I cried all night, sick from worry."

"I'm fine, Mama. I'm so happy that we're all safe."

"Every time I think about the last few hours . . ." Nellie began sobbing.

Meanwhile, Leah continued her frantic search until she heard a baby's cry. Leah shrieked because a mother knows the sound of her baby—and that was Filly's cry. She raced over to the woman who was holding the infant. He was still in his nightwear and had the same white silk scarf covering his head. When he saw his mother, he reached out for her.

"That's my baby!" Leah declared.

The woman clasped him closer to her chest and said, "How do I know he's yours?"

Leah was so stunned and emotional that she began blabbering in Polish. When she tried to speak English, her accent made it difficult to understand her. Eventually, another woman intervened and took them to see the captain of the *Carpathia*, Arthur Rostron.

The woman holding the baby told him that she was in Lifeboat 11 and as it was being lowered over the side of the ship, a crewman tossed a bundle to her. At first she thought it was a rolled-up blanket, but then it began to cry and she discovered it was an infant. She kept the baby warm under her coat. When the lifeboat arrived at the *Carpathia*, the baby was hoisted in a mailbag. Later, after the woman got on board, she claimed the child as her own, and no one questioned her. The woman told the captain, "I believe that God sent this baby to me because it was an orphan."

"But he's my flesh and blood!" insisted Leah. "I'm his mother!"

"Does he have any birthmarks or other physical characteristics that could help prove he's your son?" the captain asked.

"Yes! Yes! He has a strawberry birthmark on his chest!"

The captain took the baby from the woman's arms, unwrapped the blanket, and unbuttoned the nightwear.

There on the left side of the baby's chest was a small reddish birthmark. The captain handed Filly to Leah and said, "Here's your son."

Later that day, Ruth found Leah sitting in the lounge, caressing Filly. "You found him!" Ruth said. "See, I told you he'd be safe."

When Leah explained what had happened to Filly, Ruth couldn't help but shake her head. "He was in Lifeboat 11? My mother, sister, and brother were in that boat, too! From now on, eleven will be our lucky number."

Ruth and her family continued on their journey to Benton Harbor, Michigan, where her father joined them the following year. She finished high school and graduated from Wooster College, becoming a high school teacher in Kansas. She got married and raised three children. Divorced after 20 years, she moved back to Benton Harbor and continued teaching there.

For many years, Ruth refused to talk about the Titanic. In fact, during their early childhood, her own kids didn't know that she was a survivor. Only after she retired in 1971 and moved to Santa Barbara, California, did she grant interviews and attend Titanic Historical Society conventions.

In March 1990, Ruth took her first ocean voyage since 1912, a cruise to Mexico. She died four months later at age 90. She was survived by two children, eight grandchildren, and fourteen great-grandchildren. Her ashes were scattered over the wreck of the Titanic.

Her mother, Nellie, was emotionally traumatized by the Titanic disaster and always cried whenever the subject was brought up. Nellie died in 1961 at age 85. Ruth's sister, Marion, was only 37 when she died of tuberculosis in 1944. Richard, who was widowed twice, had a varied career as a singer, social worker, and safety inspector. He died in 1975 at age 65 and was survived by two daughters and seven grandchildren.

Leah Aks and her son, Filly, were reunited with her husband, Sam, and put down roots in Norfolk, Virginia, where he gave up tailoring for the scrap-metal business. Leah was so grateful to Captain Arthur Rostron of the Carpathia for her rescue—and for helping her get Filly back—that she named her only daughter Sarah Carpathia Aks. (Because of a miscommunication at the hospital, the baby girl's original birth certificate read "Sarah Titanic Aks.") Leah also had another son, Henry. She died in 1967 at age 73.

Frank Philip "Filly" Aks became known as the "Titanic baby" in the press. When he was still a teenager, he joined his father's scrap-metal business (which he eventually took over), married, and raised a family. He collected Titanic mementoes and attended several survivor conventions. He died in 1991 at age 80.

The wealthy woman who covered Filly's head with an off-white silk scarf when passengers were abandoning ship reportedly was Madeleine Astor, the 18-year-old bride of the famous millionaire John Jacob Astor IV.

The white silk scarf and the plaid wool lap blanket from Lifeboat 11 have remained in the possession of the Aks family ever since the tragedy. The items were put on display at the Mariners' Museum in Newport News, Virginia.

"How Will Anyone Find Us?"

William "Willie" Coutts Jr.

To nine-year-old Willie Coutts, the *Titanic* was a giant floating playground. Even though he was traveling in third class, which didn't have nearly the luxuries as first or second class, he turned every day into a fun day.

He made friends with a group of English-speaking boys around his own age, and together they roamed throughout the ship, exploring its wonders—except for places that were off-limits to all but the wealthy passengers. The boys didn't mind. Who needed a fancy gymnasium when they could hang from baggage cranes and climb ladders? So what if they weren't allowed in the Turkish baths? They had access to the steamy engine room. Who cared about the music recitals in the first-class lounge? The third-class lads preferred listening to the engine-room workers striking their coal shovels on the furnace grates in time with their singing.

It didn't matter to Willie and his friends that the first-class passengers ate lobster and roast beef at the elegant à la Carte Restaurant or Café Parisien. Third-class dining was pretty nice, too. They ate in two large rooms where uniformed stewards served meals on long boarding-house-style tables covered in white cloths. And the food tasted great—corned beef, fish, rabbit, steak and kidney pie, soups, puddings, and fresh-baked bread.

For Willie, the voyage was the trip of a lifetime. Like all his new buddies, London-born Willie Coutts (pronounced Kootz) was moving to America with family. He, his mother, Mary—who went by the name "Minnie"—and his three-year-old brother, Neville, were on their way to join his father, William Sr., in Brooklyn, New York. As a skilled engraver of precious metals, William had gone ahead to establish his own business and to prepare a home for the family.

William had sent Minnie money to buy second-class passage for her and the boys. But she booked the trio into a cheaper third-class cabin instead, figuring the difference she saved would be better spent toward their new American home.

Third-class accommodations were located in the lower decks and filled almost exclusively with immigrants. Those who couldn't afford cabins could go steerage, cheaper dormitory-style areas near the bow for the men and aft for the women. Willie enjoyed the mix of passengers in third class. He liked hearing all the strange-sounding languages of people who had left homelands in faraway places such as China, Russia, Sweden, and Turkey, and European countries such as France, Italy, Greece, and Germany.

Most everyone in third class had said good-bye to the only life they had ever known for one they hoped would be much better. Many women and children were going to reunite with husbands and fathers who had left for America months, even years, earlier. Waiting for some single women were fiancés or new jobs as maids and nannies.

The majority of third-class passengers came from Ireland, Scotland, and England, so it was pretty easy for Willie to join a pack of boys who spoke English.

Among them was William Johnston, eight, who left England with his parents, Andrew and Eliza, and sister, Catherine, seven. They were going to settle in Connecticut, where his father, a master plumber, hoped to start his own business.

There was Harold Goodwin, nine, also from England, who boarded the ship with his parents, Frederick and Augusta, and his siblings—Lilian, 16, Charles, 14, William, 11, Jessie, 10, and his baby brother, Sidney. His father, an electrical engineer, planned to work at a power station in Niagara Falls, New York.

The Goodwins were scheduled to cross the Atlantic on a modest steamer operating out of Southampton. But because of the coal strike, they were transferred to the *Titanic*.

Joining the group were James van Billiard, ten, and his brother Walter, nine. They were traveling with their father, Austin, an American, who was bringing the two boys from England to Pennsylvania to visit grandparents they had never met before. The three of them were coming two weeks earlier than planned to surprise them. Willie loved hearing the boys' stories about their childhood. They had spent most of the previous six years in central Africa, living in a tent with their family while their father mined for diamonds in what is now the Democratic Republic of Congo. Their mother cooked over an open fire and washed clothes by beating them against the rocks in a stream. The family eventually moved to London, where their mother was from. For the voyage, she stayed behind with their two younger siblings.

The pack also included Albert Rice, ten, and his brother George, eight. They were on their way to Spokane, Washington, with their mother, Margaret, and their three younger brothers, Eric, seven, Arthur, four, and Eugene, two. The boys' father, William, had been a machinist on the Great Northern Railway. In 1910, just four months after Eugene's birth, William was crushed to death beneath the wheels of a locomotive in a freak accident. Their widowed mother then took her children to her native Ireland. After receiving a settlement, she decided to return to Spokane with her sons.

And then there was Frankie Goldsmith, nine, who was traveling with his parents, Frank Sr. and Emily. The family was bound for Detroit, where Frank, a toolmaker and lathe operator, was hoping to find a job in the expanding auto industry. Accompanying the Goldsmiths were Thomas Theobald, a coworker of Frank's who was eager to seek his fortune in the United States, and teenager Alfred Rush, a family friend who planned to live with his older brother in Detroit.

Willie and his group gathered each morning in search of fun—and a little innocent mischief. They played in the open areas forward on D Deck and aft on B Deck. They chased each other on companionways and in passageways. And more than once they were kicked out of the men's smoking lounge and certain areas that were off-limits to third-class passengers.

The boys devised various games of skill and daring. How high could they climb a crane? How far could they tightrope-walk across a cable without falling? Who could scale a ladder with one hand the fastest? Who could stand the longest on one leg on a bollard?

If anyone was known as the daredevil, it was

Frankie. He accepted most any challenge—and sometimes suffered the consequences. Take Sunday evening,
for instance, when Frankie and his mother arrived in
the dining saloon while everyone else was eating.

"Why are you so late?" Willie asked Frankie.

"Because of you."

"Me? What did I do?"

"You triple-dared me to go hand-over-hand on that
real high cable, so I had to do it and I got grease all over
my hands. I couldn't get it off. My mum was furious and
had to get some kind of special soap and then she made
me scrub my hands over and over—at least five times."

Willie laughed and said, "That's what you get for
showing off."

"Laugh all you want. But I was the only lad who
made it across the cable."

After dinner, Willie and his friends celebrated the
birthday of Alfred Rush, who turned 16, which, in those
days, was a rite of passage to manhood. No longer in
knickers like all the younger boys, Alfred proudly wore
long pants for the first time.

That night Willie was sound asleep in his berth
when he was shaken awake by his mother, Minnie.
Through squinted eyes he saw a look of alarm on her
face, so he jumped out of bed and asked, "What's the
matter, Mummy?"

"I don't want you to be scared, but there's something

wrong with the ship. We struck an iceberg, and it must be serious because I heard some talk about lifeboats. You must get dressed right now. It's very cold outside so dress warm."

While his mother was trying to wake up Neville, who was a sound sleeper, Willie put on his knickers, thick socks, a shirt, wool sweater, and a heavy coat. He didn't have a stocking cap, so he plopped a straw hat on his head. Neville finally woke up and wasn't at all happy that his mother had interrupted his sleep. He whimpered the entire time that Minnie got him ready.

She found two life vests in the cabin and put them on the boys, adjusting the straps so they fit snuggly on them. "This probably looks scary to you, but it's merely a safety measure," she said.

"Where is yours, Mummy?" Willie asked.

"I can't find any more in our cabin, but I don't need one anyway. Come, we must go up on the deck."

Minnie led the way while holding on to the hand of little Neville, who was crying because he was frightened by all the turmoil in the corridors. Willie couldn't imagine that this great ship could sink, so he viewed this late-night episode as another interesting adventure. From their cabin near the stern deep in the ship, it took a long time to find the right passageways because some had been closed off by locked gates. The family was slowed down by corridors and stairs crowded with immigrants, some lugging suitcases and duffel bags that contained all their worldly possessions.

When the Couttses finally reached the Boat Deck, it was about 1:30 A.M. The ship was listing to port and slanting to the fore. Passengers were beginning to shove and push their way toward the few remaining lifeboats that had yet to be launched. Minnie stopped and looked left and right, fretting, "Oh, dear. I don't know where to go!"

Seeing that Minnie seemed bewildered, a crewman went up to her and said, "Hurry now, ma'am. All women and children to the lifeboats!"

"Which one?"

"Follow me." He led Minnie and the two boys to the port side toward Lifeboat 2.

"I don't have a life vest," said Minnie. "Do you know where I can get one?"

"It's too late. You'll have to get into the lifeboat without one," the seaman said.

A well-dressed man overheard the conversation and stepped forward. "Take my vest, madam," he told her. He removed his hat and the life jacket that he had strapped to himself. After he gave it to her, he put a hand on each boy's head and said, "If I go down, please pray for me."

"Oh, we will," Minnie said, putting on the life vest. "And thank you, thank you so much!"

After seeing the sadness in the man's eyes and hearing his distressing words, Willie felt nervous for the first time on the voyage. The boy began to think that the ship really could end up at the bottom of the ocean and that people, lots of people, could end up dead.

When it was the Couttses' turn to enter Lifeboat 2, First Officer William Murdoch helped Minnie get in and then lifted Neville and practically tossed him into her arms. Willie started to enter when Murdoch put his hand on the boy's chest and stopped him. "Where do you think you're going?" the officer said.

"In the boat with my mother and brother."

"Children only," Murdoch growled.

"But he *is* a child!" Minnie shouted. "Let him in!"

"He looks too old."

"I'm only nine," Willie said.

"Willie," Minnie said, "take off your hat and let him see you're just a child."

Willie removed his straw hat so Murdoch could get a good look at the freckle-faced, redheaded boy.

"All right, get in," Murdoch said. "That hat of yours makes you look a lot older."

The boy put his straw hat back on and hopped into the boat next to his mother and brother. Once he settled in, he saw Murdoch assist whimpering first-class passenger Mrs. Mahala Douglas, of Minneapolis, into the boat. Refusing to sit down, she reached out for her husband, Walter, and begged him to come with her. But he refused, telling her, "My darling, I would be less of a man if I got in. I must remain a gentleman."

Murdoch then helped Mrs. Luise Kink-Heilmann and her four-year-old daughter, also named Luise, into the lifeboat, but he ordered the woman's husband, Anton, to step back. "You're not a child, so move away," the officer barked. Even though there was still plenty of room for at least a dozen more passengers, Murdoch ordered the crewmen who were handling the davits to "Lower away!"

Mrs. Kink-Heilmann, of Zurich, Switzerland, threw her hands in the air and wailed. Although Willie didn't understand exactly what she was saying because she was speaking German, he could tell that she wanted her husband in the boat with her. Off to the side with other men, Anton shouted back to her in a mournful voice. She shrieked even louder as the boat began to descend. Suddenly, Anton broke from the group of men, sidestepped Murdoch, leaped over the railing, and jumped into the boat. There was no way the crewmen could get him out without disrupting the launching or endangering the passengers already in the lifeboat.

When No. 2 reached the water and the falls were released, Fourth Officer Joseph Boxhall took charge. The only crewmen aboard were a seaman, a steward, and a cook, so some women helped maneuver the boat.

One handled the tiller while the others worked the oars. Willie figured the women had come from first class because they were wearing fur coats.

The lifeboat was about a quarter of a mile away from the *Titanic* when the ship went down. Willie looked around in the vast icy darkness. Other than a brilliant starlit sky, he saw nothing. No survivors, no wreckage, no lifeboats, no icebergs, no rescue ship. And suddenly he felt all alone. *How will anyone find us?* he wondered.

"If all goes well, we should be rescued before the morning light," Boxhall said. "The *Carpathia* is on her way. We're lucky. We can make her see us." The officer had several green flares, which he periodically lit, hoping to attract the rescue ship as well as other lifeboats.

Less than two hours after the *Titanic* sank, Willie and many others spotted a green rocket and heard a distant boom.

"That's the *Carpathia*!" Boxhall shouted. "She's telling us she's arrived!" He fired off the last of his green flares, which helped direct the steamer to No. 2's position. But a breeze turned the sea choppy, making it difficult to row the lifeboat.

The steamer had its own problems because it had to maneuver around several growlers and icebergs. But eventually it reached No. 2—the first lifeboat to be rescued. Once the lifeboat had been secured, Minnie squeezed Willie's hand and told him, "We're safe now."

Willie finally could relax his neck and shoulder muscles, which had become painfully tight from shivering.

Some women in the boat began crying from relief; some, though, had completely lost control by releasing their pent-up anguish. When an officer on the deck of the *Carpathia* hailed the lifeboat, Mrs. Douglas cried out to him, "The *Titanic* has gone down with everyone on board!"

"Shut up!" Boxhall scolded her. "Pull yourself together, madam."

Mrs. Douglas immediately reined in her emotions and apologized to Boxhall.

Once aboard, the Coutts family was whisked into a lounge where they were checked over by a doctor and given blankets, hot drinks, and food. At daybreak, Willie watched the unloading of several other lifeboats but didn't spot any of his pals. He assumed they had come aboard while he was in the lounge. After all the survivors were picked up and the *Carpathia* began sailing for New York, Willie searched throughout the ship for his friends. The only one he could find was Frankie Goldsmith. "Are your mum and dad safe?" Willie asked.

"My mum is," Frankie replied. "I'm still waiting for Father to show up on another rescue ship."

"Have you seen any of the other boys?"

Frankie shook his head. "You're the only one."

"What about your friend Alfred Rush?"

Frankie shrugged and said, "I don't know. We were rushing to get to the Boat Deck, but we were stopped at a gate. Only women and children were let through, so Mother and I were allowed to pass. But Father, Mr. Theobald, and Alfred stayed back. A seaman grabbed Alfred by the arm and tried to pull him through with us because, as you know, Alfred is short and doesn't look much older than us. But Alfred jerked his arm out of the seaman's hand and said, 'No, I'm staying here with the men.' Mum begged him to come with us, but he wouldn't do it. I hope he's on the same rescue ship as Father."

But there was no other rescue ship. Of the pack of boys who played together, only Willie and Frankie Goldsmith survived. All the other boys and their entire families perished.

Frankie Goldsmith's father, Frank Sr.; 16-year-old Alfred Rush; and family friend Thomas Theobald died. Frankie and his mother, Emily, went on to Detroit to pick up the pieces of their shattered lives. Emily eventually remarried and was a volunteer for the American Red Cross. She died in 1955 at the age of 75.

Frankie went to school in Detroit, got married, raised three children, and owned a photographic equipment and supply store in Mansfield, Ohio. He admitted that for years after the disaster, he half expected his father to walk through the door. Frankie died in 1982 at the age of 79. His ashes were scattered from a Coast Guard plane onto the sea over the spot where the Titanic sank. A wreath was also dropped from the plane in honor of all the victims.

After the Couttses settled in America, they did not care to speak publicly about the tragedy. Minnie died in 1960 at the age of 84. Neville eventually married and worked as a salesman in New York City. He died in Florida in 1977 at age 68.

After Willie grew up, he married, raised two daughters, and was a professional musician. In 1957, he died in Ohio of a heart attack on the way back to his car after performing in a concert. He was 55.

"They're All Going to Die!"

Robertha "Bertha" Watt

Twelve-year-old Robertha "Bertha" Watt sat in a comfy settee in the second-class lounge and opened her prized possession—her autograph album.

Pasted in its pages were photos of family and friends left behind in Aberdeen, Scotland. She and her mother, Elizabeth—whom everyone called Bessie—were heading to America on the *Titanic* to join her father in Portland, Oregon, where he had gone the year before to set up practice as an architect. Bertha's album also contained poems and farewell messages from her school chums, her gymnastics club, and members of the Belmont Congregational Church.

By Sunday, the fourth day of her voyage, her album was filling up with autographs and salutations from the many acquaintances and new friends she had made aboard the ship. The latest person to sign it was one of her fellow shipmates from second class, eight-year-old

Marjorie "Madge" Collyer, of Bishopstoke, Hampshire, England. Madge and her parents were on their way to Idaho to begin a new life as owners of an orchard.

"Thank you for signing my album, Madge," said Bertha, admiring the young girl's curlicue signature.

Bertha rested the open album on her lap and showed her friend some of the autographs she had collected. "This is Miss Marion Wright's. She's from Somerset, England, and she's going to Oregon, too, just like me. She spent months making her own trousseau and is bringing sixty wedding presents from family and friends. Her fiancé is waiting for her in New York, and they're going to get married there as soon as we arrive. Doesn't that sound heavenly? And then he's taking her to his fruit farm in Oregon."

Bertha flipped a page. "Oh, and here's an autograph from Miss Kate Buss. She's from Kent, and she's getting married, too. Her fiancé lives in California. She's brought two steamer trunks full of swell things like Irish linen sheets, hand-embroidered bedspreads and tablecloths, silver table ornaments, and even a Singer sewing machine."

On the opposite page was a neatly penned signature. "This is from Dr. Pain."

Madge giggled. "Dr. Pain? That's a funny name for a doctor. Is he pulling your leg?"

"No. Alfred Pain really is a medical doctor. He was

studying in London, and now he's returning home to Canada. He's so handsome and very smart, too. He's only twenty-three and one of the youngest surgeons in Toronto. I hear he's an excellent marksman and swimmer and cricket player. Oh, and he plays the flute beautifully. I've heard him."

Showing Madge an autograph accompanied by a line from scripture, Bertha said, "This belongs to Sidney Clarence Stuart Collett. He's an evangelist. Did you know he began preaching in the streets of London when he was only twelve? That's my age."

The next page revealed a pencil drawing of an intricate flower. "Who did that?" Madge asked.

"Isn't that beautiful? That was drawn by Mr. Leopold Weisz. He's a famous stone carver and sculptor in Canada. He and his wife, Mathilde, are an interesting couple. He's from Hungary and she's from Belgium. They met when they were students at an art school in England, and they fell in love and got married. He went to Montreal and became quite in demand, so he returned to England to bring Mrs. Weisz back with him to Canada. Have you met her? She's extraordinary. Do you know she can speak seven languages?"

"Can you speak other languages?" Madge asked.

"A little French," Bertha answered. "I use it when I talk to those two adorable little children who run around on the Promenade Deck. You've seen them.

They're the ones who look like real-life cupids."

"You mean the Hoffman boys? They are so cute. I love their curly hair and rosy cheeks."

"I feel sad for Lolo and Momon," said Bertha. "One is three and the other is two, and they have no mother. From what I heard, she died in Nice, France, and their father is taking them to America."

"Mr. Hoffman never lets them out of his sight."

Bertha closed her album and suggested, "Why don't we go play with them right now?"

Later that evening, Bertha and her mother attended a hymn-sing conducted by Rev. Carter in the dining saloon. Marion sang two solos and Mrs. Weisz sang one. Dr. Pain played the flute.

Afterward, Bertha and her mother went to their cabin. While Bessie stayed up to read, Bertha fell right to sleep. But well after midnight, she was awakened by her mother.

"Bertha, Bertha, you must get up now!" said Bessie.

The girl could tell from her mother's voice that something was wrong. She sat up, rubbed her eyes, and asked, "What is it, Mother?"

"The ship is in trouble. When I heard the engines stop, I threw on my coat, went up on deck, and asked an officer why we weren't moving. He told me to go back to bed and that we'd be on our way soon. But Mr. Collyer just informed me that there's a serious problem because they're preparing the lifeboats. He told me we need to get up on deck right away. Bertha, put on your coat . . . and say your prayers."

The girl donned her coat, which was lined in squirrel fur, over her nightclothes and slipped her feet into her bedroom slippers. Just then, Marion Wright showed up. "Have you heard?" said Marion. "The ship has hit an iceberg and it's sinking. We need to get off right now."

The three of them scampered up to the Boat Deck on the port side, where they were joined by Dr. Pain. The deck was filling up with passengers, but there was little panic. In fact, Bertha heard many people around her who didn't want to hop into any lifeboat. They believed they were safer staying on the "unsinkable" ship rather than in a tiny boat in the middle of the ocean . . . in the pitch-black night . . . in the brutal cold.

Shortly after 1 A.M., Dr. Pain insisted, "You ladies need to get in a lifeboat." Seeing how crowded it was on the port side, he led them to the starboard side, where First Officer William Murdoch was loading No. 9. "Any more ladies or little ones?" he hollered.

"Yes, I have three for you!" Dr. Pain shouted. He ushered Bertha, Bessie, and Marion over to the lifeboat and helped them board. Once they were settled, Dr. Pain stepped back, waved to them, and said, "I'll see you back here or in New York."

Noticing that there weren't enough seamen in the boat, Murdoch turned to several crewmen standing nearby and said, "You there, can you handle a boat?"

"Yes, sir," they said in unison.

"Then in you go!"

Even though the boat had room for at least another 20 people, Murdoch ordered it lowered. Like many of the lifeboats, No. 9 tipped up and down on its way to the water. When it was released from the falls and began to rock, Bertha clutched her mother's arm. "Do you think we'll be safe in this boat?"

"Nothing to fear, Bertha," said Bessie. "You weren't born to be drowned."

As No. 9 slowly pulled away, most everyone could see how low the *Titanic*'s bow was getting. Deckhand George F. "Paddy" McGough, who was manning the tiller in the stern, bellowed to his fellow seamen, "She can't be saved! Row for all you're worth, or we'll be drawn down by the suction!"

But the stewards who were rowing couldn't get No. 9 to move fast enough. "For the love of God, ladies," McGough yelled, "lend a hand or we're all doomed."

Those within reach of the oars—including Bessie—helped row until the lifeboat was a safe distance away when the *Titanic* sank.

In the darkness, Bertha couldn't see the people who had fallen or been pitched into the icy ocean. But she, like all the survivors, could hear their pitiful moans and pleas for help.

"Oh, how horrible," Bertha cried out. "They're all going to die! Can't we do something?"

"There's nothin' we can do, lassie," said McGough.

"There is one thing," said Bessie. "Pray for their souls."

Many in the boat wept. Others sat in silence, too numb physically, mentally, and emotionally to say or do anything.

"You might as well stop rowin'," McGough shouted to the rowers. "We have nowhere to go. No sense tirin' yourselves for no reason."

"Mother, what's going to happen to us?" asked Bertha, shivering from the cold and the fear of the unknown.

"Pray that a ship rescues us soon." Bessie put her arm around Bertha and, in a comforting voice, said, "Pretend this is a lovely night on Loch Ness, and we're out for a nice row."

Bertha tried to picture that pleasant thought in her mind, but there were too many distractions—especially the survivors in No. 9, who were bickering or wailing.

Nearby, the preacher Collett sat glumly with his chin on his walking stick, lamenting repeatedly, "I can't believe this has happened to me."

Someone stood up and hissed, "Happened to *you*? It's happened to *all* of us, and it's happened to *all* the unfortunates who've lost their lives."

"But I've lost all my best sermons," the preacher whined. "I spent hours and hours writing them and now they're all gone."

Mrs. Jane Herman, whose twin 24-year-old daughters, Alice and Kate, were huddled in the boat with her, stood up and berated Collett for being so self-centered. "If you can give me back my husband and son, I'll pay for your sermons!" Then, sobbing, she collapsed in the arms of her daughters, grieving over her husband, Samuel, and 14-year-old adopted son, George Sweet.

Her outburst spurred a quick apology from Collett. "Madame, I beg your forgiveness for my unseemly bout of self-pity. You have every right to flog me. I am humbled by the grief and worry that you and everyone else are feeling. May your heart pardon my selfishness and may the Lord grant mercy on us all."

"Say, how is it that you got in this lifeboat?" McGough asked the preacher.

"Just before it was lowered, I walked up and the officer in charge had drawn his revolver and said to me, 'Where do you think you're going?' I replied that I had two young ladies in my charge and felt it my duty to take care of them. The officer said, 'Get in,' and we all got in and then a moment later the boat was lowered."

McGough growled at Collett's answer. Later, trying to buoy the spirits of those in No. 9, the seaman announced, "We *will* be rescued. I heard from good authority that the *Carpathia* is steamin' to our rescue. She should be here by daybreak."

Bertha thought about all the people she had met on the *Titanic* and wondered how many of them survived. Madge. The Hoffman boys. Mr. and Mrs. Weisz. Dr. Pain. And all the interesting passengers who were kind enough to sign her album. *My album! Oh, how I wish I had brought it with me. Now it's lost forever.* But she didn't dare complain, not after witnessing the emotional exchange between Mrs. Herman and Collett.

No. 9 had no lights, water, matches, or compass. The only supplies in the lifeboat were cookies in a tin, which were passed around for those who felt like eating. Food didn't interest Bertha in the least. She was much too nervous. "Without a compass, will we get lost?" she asked McGough.

"No, lassie," he said. "We have the North Star."

"Where's that?"

"You see that groupin' of stars?" he said, pointing to the constellation known as the Big Dipper. "Now follow an imaginary line from the two stars farthest from the handle. You see that bright one over there? That's the North Star. It's always due north. That star has guided many a sea captain over the years."

Through the night, McGough kept up a running monologue on everything from navigation to Irish whiskey to life on the sea. Shortly before dawn, he stopped in midsentence. "Did you see that?" he shouted, pointing to green flashes coming from the southeast. "Those are rockets from the *Carpathia*. Let us all pray to God, for there is a ship on the horizon, and she's makin' for us!"

As more flares were fired, Bertha could hear cheers coming from other lifeboats that were still too far away to be seen in the dark. But soon the gray light of dawn revealed the *Titanic*'s lifeboats scattered over several square miles among dozens of small icebergs and a few massive ones that towered more than 200 feet high.

When it was No. 9's turn to come alongside the *Carpathia*, a Jacob's ladder was lowered right in front of Bertha. "Go ahead," Bessie told her. "You can climb that."

Even though she could barely feel anything with her hands because they were so frozen, Bertha gripped the rope ladder and began scaling it.

"Don't let anyone up without a safety belt on!" an officer on the ship yelled down to the seamen in the lifeboat. Bertha was climbing without one, but she refused to return to the boat to put one on, not when she was so close to getting on the ship. Being the athletic girl that she was, she reached the deck in no time.

"Oh, it feels so good to be on a ship again!" she declared as a blanket was draped over her shoulders and she was handed a hot toddy. It was the first time her lips had ever sipped an alcoholic drink. She liked the warmth but not the burning sensation in her stomach.

Looking out from the deck, she saw lifeboats heading to the *Carpathia* from all directions. Combined with the big bergs and smaller growlers, it looked like a regatta. Beyond the lifeboats, as far as she could see to the north and west, was an endless ice field.

The survivors arrived in all manner of dress. Some in evening clothes, robes, kimonos, and fur coats. Some in bare feet, satin slippers, laced-up boots, and patent leather shoes. Some in wide-brimmed bonnets, woolen stocking caps, tweed hats, and knitted scarves.

Bertha was relieved to spot Madge and Mrs. Weisz and several other women who had signed her autograph book earlier. But too many others whose signatures were in her album were still missing.

She was too exhausted to stay on the deck any longer to watch who came aboard. With her mother, she went into a lounge that was getting crowded with blanket-wrapped survivors curled up in chairs, lying on the floor, and sprawled on tabletops.

In the corner, a group of women were huddled around a toddler who was crying. Occasionally, he blurted out a word that sounded French. Bertha couldn't quite make it out, so she went over to the women and peeked over their shoulders.

"Why, that's Momon!" she said.

"You know this little boy?" one of the women asked.

"Yes, he's Momon Hoffman. He was on the *Titanic* with his older brother, Lolo, and their father." Bertha kneeled down and got him to stop crying. In French, she asked him, "Where is Lolo? Where is your father?"

Momon began wailing again. Bertha finally figured out that he was scared because he had been separated from his brother and father. "Let's go find them," she said. Holding the hand of the sniffling little boy, Bertha joined two other women who walked around the ship, asking survivors if they had seen Mr. Hoffman or Lolo. She soon learned that Margaret Hays, a first-class passenger who spoke fluent French, was taking care of Lolo in a stateroom. The two brothers were soon reunited. But their father remained among the missing.

Bertha returned to the lounge, where she found space under a table and tried to go to sleep. There was little talking now among the survivors—mostly women—but there was much crying over the loss of their husbands. All the lifeboats had been accounted for, which meant that most of the women were now widows. Mrs. Weisz was bawling so hard she was on the verge of passing out.

Bessie tucked Bertha tightly in her blanket and said,

"Go to sleep, child. I'm going to try to calm down Mrs. Weisz."

Bessie spent hours comforting the woman. With arms locked, they walked up and down the deck as the grieving widow poured out her heart over losing Leopold. After Bertha woke up from her nap, she noticed a dramatic improvement in Mrs. Weisz's emotional state. "She seems so much better," Bertha told her mother. "How did you do that?"

"First, I let her cry on my shoulder," Bessie explained. "I let her release her anger and sorrow. Then I told her that because of her skill with languages she was desperately needed to help other widows like herself. There are many persons who don't speak English and in need of someone to translate for them."

For the rest of the voyage to New York, Mrs. Weisz put her ability to speak seven languages to good use, comforting immigrants and helping them communicate with crewmembers. At every meal, she sat at a big table of non-English-speaking women and children and ordered for them. Even though her own heart was breaking, she found relief by helping others.

Bertha didn't have to spend the night sleeping under a table. Some crewmen gave up their quarters for her, Bessie, Marion Wright, and Kate Buss.

Because Bertha and Bessie had only nightclothes under their coats, Bessie stitched together crude skirts made out of blankets for themselves. Many survivors—the wealthy and the poor alike—formed teams to sew makeshift clothing out of tablecloths, blankets, sheets, and quilts for those who had little to wear. Everyone was grateful to have clothes and even traded good-natured barbs over some of their improvised outfits.

When the *Carpathia* arrived in New York, Bertha and Bessie were met by Bessie's brother, Harry Milne, who lived near the docks. The family remained at the pier while Marion went looking for her fiancé, Arthur Woolcott. But after searching for him in the massive crowd, she returned to the Watts totally crestfallen. "I can't find Arthur anywhere," she moaned.

"Marion, you will stay with us in New York until you find him," Bessie said.

The following day, Milne began telephoning the city's hotels, hoping to find Woolcott. Milne soon discovered that he was staying at the Grand Union Hotel and left a message. Later that day at Milne's home, Woolcott and Marion rushed into each other's arms.

"I don't know how I missed you," he told Marion. "When people started to disembark, I looked for you. When the last survivor came off the ship and I didn't find you, I had the most terrible thought—that the list of survivors was wrong and that you had died. I ran aboard and was told that you indeed had been on the

Carpathia. An officer suggested that maybe you had been taken directly to a hospital. So this morning, I visited the hospitals, looking for you. When I returned to the hotel, I can't tell you how relieved and happy I was to learn that you were safe. And now, here I am . . . with you."

There would be no waiting. For Marion and her fiancé, the *Titanic* disaster was a powerful message that life is too short. They rushed down to City Hall for a marriage license. The next morning, Bertha, her mother, and her uncle accompanied the couple to St. Christopher's Chapel. In front of an altar adorned with white roses, asparagus ferns, and Easter lilies, Arthur Woolcott and Marion Wright exchanged wedding vows. Marion was given away by Milne while Bessie acted as the matron of honor.

"At least something good came out of this tragedy," Bertha told her mother after the ceremony. "I got to attend a very sweet wedding."

The day after the wedding, Marion and Arthur Woolcott left for Cottage Grove, Oregon, where they lived on an 80-acre fruit farm. They raised three sons and remained lifelong friends with Bessie and Bertha. Marion died in 1965 at age 80.

Bessie reunited with her husband in Portland, Oregon, where she lived for the rest of her life. Because of her friendship with Marion, she attended the births of Marion's three sons, who called her Grandma Watt. She died in 1951 at age 79.

Bertha graduated college and married dentist Leslie Marshall. They moved to Vancouver, British Columbia, where they raised two sons, and she became a Canadian citizen. She didn't let her Titanic experience stop her from enjoying the sea. She and her husband sailed the coastal waters of the Pacific throughout their married life. Bertha, who seldom talked about the tragedy, died in 1993 at age 93.

A month after arriving in America, Kate Buss married Samuel Willis in San Diego, California, where they raised a daughter. Kate eventually moved to Oregon, where she died in 1972 at age 96.

Mathilde Weisz lost all her money when the Titanic sank. She went to Montreal, anyway, only to learn that she would be deported from Canada because she was considered a penniless immigrant. But then the body of her husband, Leopold, was recovered. Sewn into the lining of his jacket was $15,000 worth of gold, which was turned over to Mathilde, who decided to stay in Montreal. In 1914, she married her late husband's business partner, Edward Wren, and embarked on a singing career. She died in 1953 at age 79.

Lolo and Momon Hoffman were called by the press "The Orphans of the Deep" and the "Titanic Tots" because they were parentless following the death of their father, Louis Hoffman. Or so everyone thought. But eventually the truth was revealed. The boys' real names were Michel and Edmond Navratil, sons of Michel and Marcelle Navratil, of Nice, France.

The boys, whose parents had separated, lived with their mother. On Easter Sunday 1912, their father whisked them away. Using fake names, he booked passage for the three of them on the Titanic, hoping for a fresh start in the United States. On the ship, he told people that he was a widower.

On the night of the sinking, Navratil dressed the boys and brought them to the Boat Deck, where crewmembers had locked arms around Lifeboat D so that only women and children could get through. Navratil handed the boys through the ring of men. As he placed his sons in the care of strangers, Navratil told little Michel, "My child, when your mother comes for you, as she surely will, tell her that I loved her dearly and still do."

The frightened toddlers held each other for comfort through the night. But they became separated when they were hoisted aboard the Carpathia. Each boy was placed in the arms of a different passenger and taken away. Traumatized by their ordeal and their separation, Michel and Edmond sobbed uncontrollably for their father and each other. With the help of Bertha and other passengers, the boys were eventually reunited.

The "Titanic Tots," who remained in the care of first-class passenger Margaret Hays, of New York, made front-page news around the world. In Nice, France, their distraught mother, Marcelle Navratil, read the article and soon proved the boys were not orphans but her own flesh and blood. The White Star Line then gave her free passage to New York. Any doubts that Marcelle was their mother were erased when the boys raced into her outstretched arms and cried tears of happiness. The three returned to France.

Their father's body was the fifteenth victim recovered from the ocean by the search ship Mackay-Bennett. He was buried in Halifax, Nova Scotia.

When Edmond grew up, he married and became an architect and builder. During World War II, he enlisted in the French army. He was captured in Nazi-occupied France and sent to a prisoner of war camp, but he escaped. His health declined and he died in 1953 at age 43.

Michel went on to become a scholar and teacher of philosophy. Married to a fellow philosophy student, he received his doctorate in 1952 and served as a professor at the University of Montpellier in France until his retirement in 1969. In 1996, Michel visited the grave of his father for the first and only time. He died five years later at age 92. Michel was the last living male survivor of the Titanic.

"I Can't Leave Her Behind!"

William "Billy" Carter

Eleven-year-old William "Billy" Carter kneeled down on the slanting deck of the *Titanic* and hugged his cherished dog—a tan and black Airedale terrier. "It's going to be all right, girl," Billy said. He ran his fingers through the black saddle-shaped marking that covered the back and sides of her wiry coat.

For nearly an hour, Billy, his 13-year-old sister, Lucile, and their parents, William Ernest Carter and Lucile Polk Carter, had been waiting patiently in the cold for lifeboat instructions from the ship's officers. At first they had been told that although the ship had struck an iceberg, there was no danger to the passengers. Then they were told that as a precaution, women and children would be put in lifeboats. But as the crisis grew worse, and the bow kept sinking lower, they knew they were in a life-and-death situation.

Despite the tension swirling around them, Billy

wasn't flustered because he had his best buddy, his constant companion, by his side. And she was calm, which made him calm.

Back home at the Carters' sprawling family estate, Gwenda, in Bryn Mawr, Pennsylvania, at their apartment in Philadelphia, and at their beach house in Newport, Rhode Island, the boy and his dog were nearly inseparable. The dog traveled with Billy everywhere and had made several transatlantic crossings during the Carters' frequent European vacations. His sister Lucile had her own dog on board, a cute tan and white Cavalier King Charles spaniel.

Prior to this voyage, the Carters had spent the winter at a rented estate called Rotherby Manor in a quaint country village nestled among the hunting grounds of southern England. While Mr. Carter—a world-class polo player and a skilled sportsman—engaged in his competitions, young Billy played tennis on the estate's clay court, rode horses, and played in the woods with his dog. Lucile and her mother had visited various boarding schools in search of the one that would best suit the girl.

The Carters had timed their return to the United States so they could travel on the *Titanic*'s maiden voyage. When they arrived at Southampton to board the ship, Mr. Carter personally supervised the loading of the family's many steamer trunks. His wardrobe included 60 shirts, 15 pairs of shoes, and two tuxedos with tails. He also was shipping home a new French-built automobile, called a Renault, that had been taken apart and crated for easier storage in the forward cargo hold.

Once on board, the Carters had settled into adjoining first-class staterooms on B Deck. While their parents were in one cabin, Billy and Lucile shared another with their mother's French-born maid, Auguste Serreplan. Mr. Carter's valet, Alexander Cairns, was in a separate first-class cabin while the family chauffeur, Augustus Aldworth, stayed in a second-class room.

Although the ship had kennels for passengers' dogs, there was no way that Billy and his sister were putting their pets in cages. No, the terrier and the spaniel would stay with them. The shipping line let dog owners in first class keep pets in their staterooms, although some owners chose to board their dogs in the ship's kennels.

During the voyage, Billy was often seen walking his dog on the Promenade Deck. About the only time he wasn't with the Airedale was when he was eating meals in the dining saloon. Billy and his dog spent time playing with another Airedale named, of all things, Kitty. She belonged to Colonel John Jacob Astor IV, one of the wealthiest men in the world and a friend of the Carters.

On Sunday evening, Billy and Lucile ate dinner with Miss Serreplan. They had heard that someone was trying to organize a dog show for Monday, and they were eager to parade their pets in front of the passengers.

Meanwhile, their parents had joined an exclusive dinner party held in honor of the *Titanic*'s captain, Edward J. Smith, in the swank à la Carte Restaurant. The gathering was hosted by millionaire banker and businessman George Widener and his wife, Eleanor, ("Nellie" to her friends). The guest list included, among others, Colonel Astor and his 18-year-old pregnant wife, Madeleine, and John and Marian Thayer.

Billy's parents were well-known in high society. His grandfather, William Thornton Carter, after whom he was named, made a fortune in the coal industry. Billy's father, who went by the name of Billy rather than the more formal William, inherited millions. But he didn't care much about the family business and instead put his energies in the social scene and his polo team, the Bryn Mawr Benedicts. Billy's mother was a stunning beauty who came from a wealthy Baltimore family.

After the party was over, the ladies returned to their staterooms and Captain Smith went back to the bridge. Billy's father and the other men moved over to the smoking lounge, where they played cards, chatted, and sipped nightcaps.

At 11:40 P.M., Billy, Lucile, and Miss Serreplan were

sound asleep when they were jostled awake by a tremendous thump. At first, Billy thought he was dreaming, but then he noticed that his dog had jerked to her feet. "What was that, girl?" he asked.

Lucile had awakened, too, along with her little dog. "The engines have stopped," she said. "Do you think something is wrong?"

"Oh, I'm sure it's nothing much," said Miss Serreplan.

But within minutes, Billy's mother burst into the room. "We've had a little accident," she announced. "Everybody needs to get dressed quickly."

"What happened, Mama?" Billy asked.

"Your father came down from the smoking lounge and informed me that we've struck an iceberg. He said to put on our warm clothes and we should bring our life vests just to be on the safe side. We're going to meet him in the lounge. Now, be a brave boy and get ready."

"I'm not afraid, Mama." He rubbed his dog's head and said, "And you aren't either, are you, girl?"

Once everyone was dressed, Billy hooked a leash to his Airedale's collar and said, "I'm taking her with me."

But Lucile decided against bringing her dog, saying, "It's so cold outside, she'll just freeze out there."

They hurried up to the port side of the Promenade Deck, where they were joined by the Thayers, Wideners, Astors, and another Philadelphia family, the Ryersons. The annoying roar from the funnels' steam vents made it difficult to carry on a conversation. Billy was concerned the loud noise was hurting his dog's ears, so he covered them with his hands. No one seemed particularly worried, believing that at the worst, the watertight compartments in the hull would keep the ship afloat long enough for other ships to arrive and take off all the passengers.

Eventually, an officer told the group to go up the crew's stairway to the Boat Deck. Billy noticed the ship was listing to port and was pitched downward at the bow. More alarming to him was seeing lifeboats being loaded and lowered. He wasn't concerned about getting into one. He was concerned the crew wouldn't let him take his dog with him.

"Do we really have to get in a lifeboat, Papa?" Billy asked. "Can't we just stay here on the ship until help arrives?"

His father said, "No, son. They're putting all the women and children into boats, so we have to do what they say."

No one said anything about dogs, Billy thought. *I'll just put her in the lifeboat with me.*

Lucile teared up. "Papa, what about my dog? She's all alone back in the cabin."

"Let's not worry about her," he said. "She's fine where she is—out of the cold and away from the crowd."

After waiting for more than an hour, the group was

finally led back to the Promenade Deck, where No. 4 was ready for loading through a large open window. When Second Officer Charles Lightoller saw the Airedale, he said gruffly, "No dogs!"

"But—but she's my pal," Billy blurted. "She goes everywhere with me."

"No dogs!" Lightoller said impatiently as he began helping others into the boat.

His eyes welling up, Billy turned to his mother. "Mama? Please, can we take her?"

"I'm afraid we can't do that, dear."

Turning to his father, Billy pleaded, "Papa, tell him. We can't leave her here. She's scared and she'll be alone."

His father shook his head and said, "There's nothing I can do, son."

Meanwhile, Astor helped his young pregnant wife into the lifeboat and asked Lightoller, "She's in a delicate condition. May I join her?"

"No, sir," replied the officer. "No men are allowed until all the women and children are loaded first."

Astor nodded and stepped back without a word. He joined the rest of the men in the group who were waving good-bye to their wives and loved ones. The men remained composed, believing there were other ships in the area steaming to their rescue.

Seeing Billy still begging to let the Airedale get into

the boat, Astor turned to the teary-eyed boy and said, "Lad, I'll look after your dog. She can keep Kitty company until help arrives. You'll be back together in no time. How does that sound?"

Billy burst out crying. "I can't . . . leave . . . her behind," he bawled between sobs.

"Son, you must," his father said sternly. "You're wasting precious time."

"Yes, Papa." Billy buried his head in his dog's neck and wept. "It'll be okay, girl," he whispered. "I love you." Then he reluctantly handed the leash over to Astor.

"Don't fret, lad," Astor said. "Kitty and I will take real good care of her."

"There's not a single moment to lose!" shouted Lightoller. "Hurry up, ladies!"

Marian Thayer and Eleanor Widener kissed their husbands good-bye and, along with their maids, got into the boat. Steerage women and their babies climbed in, too.

As the Carters were ready to step into the boat, steward George Dodd, who had been assisting women and children into No. 4, barked, "No more boys!"

"Oh, yes, there will be," Billy's mother muttered under her breath. She took off her wide feathered hat and plopped it on the boy's head. Grabbing his hand, she yanked him into the boat with her. His sister, Lucile, and Miss Serreplan also got in.

Even though the boat was only half full, Lightoller shouted, "Lower away!"

As the boat began its descent, Billy caught a last glimpse of his beloved Airedale. The dog strained against the leash and yelped as if she wanted to jump into the boat. The sight tore at his heart. Even when he no longer could see her, Billy could hear her high-pitched barks. It hurt so much to leave her behind.

The boat jerked and seesawed on its way down until it smacked into the water. "How many seamen do you have?" Lightoller shouted from above.

"Only one!" shouted seaman Willy McCarthy. "Me!"

"That's not enough. I'll send you another."

From the Boat Deck, quartermaster Walter Perkis slid down one of the falls and dropped into No. 4. "Release the lines, or we'll get sucked down with the ship!" he shouted. Once the boat was freed, it remained only a few yards away from the *Titanic*. With only two seamen, there weren't enough men to handle the oars. So Mrs. Carter—along with Marian Thayer, Madeleine Astor, and several other women who had never touched an oar in their lives—pitched in and rowed.

Billy was still crying over being separated from his dog. With all the room in the boat, he couldn't understand why his Airedale couldn't be by his side . . . or why his father and the other men were left behind.

After the *Titanic* sank, No. 4 was in the best position

to pick up survivors. Against the wishes of certain women who feared the lifeboat would get swamped, those manning the oars rowed toward several swimmers. About a dozen crewmen in the water—some so frozen they could barely move—were hauled in.

Billy kept peering in the darkness, hoping against hope that the next swimmer he spotted would be his father or his Airedale. But each time he saw movement in the water, it turned out to be another struggling crewman.

Throughout the frigid night, Billy tolerated the cold because he was dressed warmly and wearing his mother's hat. His mind stayed focused on ways in which his father and dog could have survived the sinking. *Maybe Papa made it into another lifeboat. Maybe they're floating on a raft. Maybe she's still paddling out there somewhere.* Yes, the 28-degree water was not survivable, but in the mind of an 11-year-old heartsick boy, the dog could be alive because she was a strong swimmer, had a thick coat, and loved playing in cold weather. He ached to hold her in his arms again and he prayed that his father was safe.

His sister, Lucile, was anguished, too, not knowing her father's fate but knowing that her adorable dog had drowned in the cabin. "I feel so horrible that I left her alone with no chance to escape," she whimpered. Out of respect for the women in the boat who undoubtedly had lost husbands and sons, she said no more about her pet.

Early the next morning, the weary survivors in No. 4 finally reached the *Carpathia*. Billy looked up, searching for his father among the faces of those *Titanic* passengers who had already been picked up and were now lining the decks. His mother let out a shriek. "Billy! Billy!" she shouted, standing up and waving her arms at her husband.

"It's Papa!" squealed Lucile. "It's a miracle!" She hopped to her feet, waved and yelled, "Hi, Papa!"

From the *Carpathia*'s deck, Mr. Carter flashed a big grin that suddenly disappeared. His eyes scanned the people in the lifeboat below and, with some apprehension, shouted back, "Where's Billy? Did he make it? Is he safe? Where's Billy?"

Realizing that his mother's big feathered hat had covered his face, Billy whipped it off, stood up, and yelled, "Here I am, Papa!"

Minutes later, Billy, Lucile, and their parents were hugging each other, incredibly thankful that the entire family had survived when so few had. Although thrilled that the Carter clan was safe, Billy needed to know: "Papa, where's my dog?"

"Son, I don't know. The last I saw of Colonel Astor, he was heading aft with her. I haven't seen them since." Putting his hands on Billy's shoulders and looking straight into the boy's eyes, he said, "Son, there are only a few lifeboats left to get picked up. You have to prepare yourself for the strong possibility that she is . . ."

Billy put his hands to his ears, closed his eyes, and howled, "I don't want to hear that!"

"Papa, how did you get here?" Lucile asked. "We were so worried you went down with the ship."

"When I left you, I ran over to the starboard side of the Boat Deck," Mr. Carter explained. "There I saw Mr. Ismay and several officers filling the boats with women and children, mostly from steerage. I aided them in the work, and as the last boat was being filled we looked around for more women. I guess there were about forty of them in the boat. Mr. Ismay and I and several of the officers walked up and down the deck, shouting, 'Are there any more women here?' We called for several minutes and got no answer.

"One of the officers then declared that we could get into the boat if we would help row with two seamen. Mr. Ismay called again and after we got no reply, we got into the lifeboat and rowed. We were about a mile away from the *Titanic* when I watched her go down. Mr. Ismay refused to look. He hardly spoke at all, he was so distraught.

"Throughout the night, all I kept thinking about was you. I feared for your lives, not knowing how you fared after you left in the lifeboat."

"We Carters are so lucky," said Mrs. Carter. "We all survived."

Billy's Airedale terrier and Lucile's Cavalier King Charles spaniel were never found. Of the ten dogs believed to be aboard the Titanic, only three lapdogs—two Pomeranians and a Pekinese—survived because they were smuggled into lifeboats by their owners.

When the Carter family arrived in New York, Mr. Carter told reporters, "No pen can ever depict and no tongue can ever describe adequately the terrors of our experience. Everywhere was cold, hopeless despair and grief. . . ."

The family learned that Mr. Carter's valet, Alexander Cairns, and chauffeur, Augustus Aldworth, had perished.

Like J. Bruce Ismay, Mr. Carter experienced withering criticism for getting into a lifeboat when so many others couldn't or wouldn't. Many of his wealthy friends—the most important figures in business and industry—had died. As a consequence, high society in Philadelphia and Newport shunned him and Mrs. Carter.

Two years later, she filed for divorce, claiming that her husband had "deserted" her and the children and jumped into a different lifeboat before theirs was launched. Although it wasn't true—it was later determined he left in Lifeboat C five to ten minutes after Lifeboat 4 was launched—Mr. Carter had to live with that stigma until his death in 1940. Young Billy knew the truth and sided with his father. Two months after his mother was granted a divorce, she married George Brooke, a wealthy Philadelphian.

According to a family friend, Billy's mother remained emotionally traumatized by the Titanic tragedy and became increasingly eccentric over the years. She died in 1934 at age 59.

His sister, Lucile, married Samuel J. Reeves and raised two children. She died in 1962 at age 64, leaving behind six grandchildren.

Billy never married and died in Bryn Mawr, Pennsylvania, in 1985 at age 84. He was buried alongside his father, who never remarried, in a huge mausoleum at West Laurel Hill Cemetery in Bala Cynwyd, Pennsylvania.

Billy seldom talked about the Titanic and made a point of avoiding researchers and others who were interested in learning more about his story. A family friend said Billy's reluctance to discuss the disaster stemmed from his lifelong heartache over losing his cherished dog.

"Please Don't Shoot Him!"

Marjorie "Madge" Collyer

"Oh, what an adventure we're going on!" eight-year-old Marjorie "Madge" Collyer told her cherished doll, Dolly. "Mum, Daddy, and I—and you, of course—are going to a new country. America!"

Madge cradled the doll, whose dark hair and blue eyes matched hers, and twirled around in her room. She would soon be leaving her home in Bishopstoke, Hampshire, England, for a new life in Payette, Idaho. "Daddy says we'll own an orchard and grow fruit. The summers will be warm and sunny and dry—and that will make Mum feel so much better. Isn't that just . . . just . . . divine!"

Whatever fears Madge felt about leaving, her father, Harvey, chased them away. As the only child, Madge was a "daddy's girl" who loved watching him make little figures and objects out of folded paper for her. Harvey, who owned a grocery store, doted on Madge and brought her treats and little unexpected gifts for no reason at all. Two years earlier, for Christmas, he bought Madge her favorite present of all—Dolly, which became her constant companion almost everywhere. Madge would share her secrets and dreams with Dolly as if it were her dearest friend.

The girl was also close with her mother, Charlotte, known affectionately as "Lottie" or "Lot" to family. Lottie suffered from lung infections that made it difficult for her to breathe at times, especially in the damp, gray English weather. She downplayed her illness so Madge wouldn't worry. But the little girl knew her mother was in poor health because the woman couldn't stop wheezing, coughing, and hacking. Lottie worked as a housekeeper for the vicar at St. Mary's Church, where Harvey, a lay official at the church, was responsible for the ringing of its steeple bells.

Harvey and Lottie had friends who immigrated to Payette in southwestern Idaho several years earlier and built a successful business by growing fruit. They wrote the couple glowing accounts of Payette's beauty, climate, and opportunities and urged them to seek their fortune there. The Collyers never seriously considered the idea until Lottie's lung problems took a turn for the worse. She needed to live in a warmer, drier place, so they decided to head for America, where they planned to buy a half interest in a 10-acre orchard near Payette.

Harvey sold his grocery store and bought three tickets for second-class passage on the *Titanic*. The family shipped most of their possessions ahead of their scheduled arrival.

The day before the Collyers were due to sail, hundreds of townspeople turned out to bid the family farewell. In the afternoon, members of the church arranged a surprise for Harvey. They led him to a seat under an old tree in the churchyard and then rang the bells in various melodies for more than an hour in his honor. Seeing the pleased look on her father's face, Madge felt happy for him—although she got bored after the first 20 minutes.

During the recital, Madge overheard her mother whisper to a friend, "It's almost too much of a farewell ceremony. I'd rather concentrate on where we're going rather than what we're leaving behind."

Madge's happy anticipation about moving to a new country was tempered when she had to say goodbye to her friends and both sets of grandparents in Bishopstoke. She wondered if she would ever see them again.

The next morning, the family traveled to Southampton, where Harvey withdrew from the bank all his money, including the proceeds from the sale of his store. The teller suggested Harvey use a bank draft—a check from one bank to another—because it was safer than money. But Harvey insisted on cash in American bills. He then put the family's life savings in his wallet, which he placed in the inside breast pocket of his coat.

When the Collyers arrived at the bustling dock, they felt overwhelmed by the huge size of the black-hulled ship. They were also awed by the thousands of onlookers and well-wishers who had gathered to see friends and loved ones off on the *Titanic*'s maiden voyage.

The family had never sailed before, prompting a friend at the dock to ask, "Aren't you afraid to venture out on the sea?"

"What? On this boat?" replied Lottie. "Even the worst storm couldn't harm her."

Stroking Dolly's hair, Madge piped up, "I'm not afraid. I'm excited."

After her first look around the magnificent vessel, Madge said, "It's like a floating town!"

Over the next few days, she met some of the more than two dozen children who were in second class, which had no organized activities for them. Kids had to make up their own fun.

Madge quickly made friends with 12-year-old Robertha "Bertha" Watt, of Aberdeen, Scotland. The two girls entertained themselves by exploring the ship and playing with some of the toddlers on board.

On Sunday evening, the Collyers sat down for

dinner in the second-class dining saloon. Even though they had enjoyed several meals there since Wednesday, Madge still was amazed by the fancy china, crisp linen, and courteous service. She studied the evening's menu, which featured three courses—consommé with tapioca; a choice of baked haddock, curried chicken, broiled lamb, or roast turkey; turnip sauce, peas, rice, and boiled and roasted potatoes; and for dessert, plum pudding with sweet sauce, wine jelly, coconut sandwich, or American ice cream as well as assorted nuts, fresh fruit, cheese, and cookies.

"Everything looks so good I wish I had five stomachs so I could eat it all," said Madge.

Like he did during all their meals, her father folded and twisted his napkin into the shape of an animal—this time, a lovely swan that delighted Madge.

When the meal was over, the family took a brisk walk on the Promenade Deck. The temperature had turned considerably colder, dipping into the thirties, causing them to cut their stroll short. Harvey then went into the men's-only smoking lounge, while Madge and her mother headed for their cabin. Along the way, they encountered their stewardess.

"It's so cold I have the shivers," Madge said.

"Do you know where we are?" the stewardess asked them. Before they could answer, she said, "We're in the Devil's Hole."

"What's that?" asked Madge.

"That is a dangerous part of the ocean," she answered. "Many accidents have happened there. They say that icebergs drift down as far as where we are. It's getting to be very cold on the decks, so perhaps there is ice around us now."

After the stewardess left, Madge asked, "Are you worried, Mummy?"

Lottie caressed the girl's long dark hair, smiled reassuringly, and replied, "Absolutely not. Now that we're in the Devil's Hole, the crew will be ever more vigilant in looking out for icebergs."

As Madge snuggled into bed with her doll, she said, "See, Dolly? There's nothing to worry about."

With their stomachs full, Madge and her mother fell right to sleep. At about 11 P.M., Harvey entered the cabin and after he unintentionally woke up Lottie, the two chatted for more than a half hour. Then they felt a strange sensation.

"My goodness, what was that?" said Harvey, who nearly lost his balance.

"It felt as if the ship had been seized by a giant hand and shaken," Lottie replied.

Madge sat up in bed. "The boat has stopped," she said. "I don't hear the engines anymore."

The silence was broken by the pounding of footsteps on the decks and passageways.

"Darling," Lottie said to Harvey, "be a dear and find out what is happening."

He quickly dressed and left the cabin. When he returned a short time later, Madge noticed that he looked tense. She clutched her doll and asked, "Daddy, what's wrong?"

"It seems we have hit an iceberg," Harvey announced. "They say everything will be all right, but then one of the stewards told me to gather our life vests and go up on the Boat Deck."

Lottie bolted out of bed, threw on a dressing gown and light coat, and tied her long hair into a ponytail with a ribbon. "There's no time to waste," she told Madge. Lottie helped her put a coat on over her nightclothes. Harvey then wrapped the girl in a White Star blanket and hustled his wife and daughter out of the cabin.

When they reached the Boat Deck, Madge felt the sting of the frosty air. Suddenly, she was seized with alarm. "My Dolly!" she cried. "I left Dolly on my pillow. I must go back and get her."

Harvey grasped her arm and said, "No, we can't."

"But, Daddy, I can't leave Dolly!"

"Madge, listen to me. We all left things behind. I left my watch. Mum left her rings."

"What about our money?" Lottie asked.

Harvey patted the chest pocket of his coat and said, "It's safe with me."

"What's going to happen to us?" Madge asked.

"We'll be fine," her father said. "I was told the crew is checking things over for damage. It's probably much ado about nothing. I heard that some men were playing cards when the ship hit the iceberg. Their cards fell on the floor, but they picked them up and went right on with the game. These are men who have made many ocean crossings before. If we were in any real danger, do you think they would still be playing cards? We will be fine."

Madge always believed her father, and she wanted to this time, too. But the way his voice wavered and the way his eyes glanced away from hers made the girl suspect he didn't believe his own words. She wished she was holding Dolly.

The deck was filling with alarmed passengers as stone-faced crewmen scurried about. Madge was startled to see a stoker—a man who tended one of the ship's steam boilers—emerge from belowdecks. Covered in coal dust and grimacing in pain, he held what looked like a bloody fist to his sweaty, dirty chest. Then she realized that it wasn't a fist but a hand with its fingers cut off.

"Look, that man is hurt!" shouted Madge.

Lottie asked him, "Are we in any danger?"

"Danger?" he bellowed. "I should say so! Men are drowning, and machinery is breaking loose. This boat will sink like a stone in ten minutes!"

Harvey put his arm around Lottie and she, in turn, squeezed Madge's hand. Although her father stood strong, Madge noticed that all color had drained from his face.

"It's worse than we thought," he muttered.

"Lower the boats!" shouted the officers, who were now running to their stations. "Women and children first! Women and children first!"

An officer hurried over to the Collyers and told Harvey, "The wife and child need to get into a lifeboat right now."

As Lottie secured the life jacket on Madge, the girl began to cry. "Who will look after Dolly?"

Harvey searched in his coat pocket and pulled out a piece of paper. Folding and tearing it, he created a small angel. "Let's pretend this is Dolly's guardian angel," he said. "We'll leave the angel here on the ship, and she'll watch over Dolly until we get back." He tucked the paper angel between slats of a deck chair.

Turning to his wife, he said, "Lottie, you and Madge must go."

"No, I'm not leaving without you," Lottie declared.

By now it was 1:30 A.M., and the bow of the boat was sinking at a noticeable angle. Suddenly, Madge felt two strong hands grab her around the waist and yank her away from her mother. "Mummy! Daddy!" she yelped. The hands belonged to a crewman who had picked her up and bodily threw her into Lifeboat 14, which was still attached to the davits.

The crewman returned and barked to Lottie, "You, too, lady! Take a seat in that boat or it will be too late!"

"No!" she yelled.

Two crewmen then seized her and began hustling her to No. 14.

"Go, Lottie!" Harvey shouted to her. "For God's sake, be brave and go! I'll find a seat in another boat!"

The men shoved Lottie into the lifeboat, and she landed hard on her side next to Madge. "Mummy, are you all right?" the girl asked.

"I've bruised my shoulder." As more women were being tossed into the boat, Lottie wobbled to her feet, hoping to catch a glimpse of her husband. She spotted the back of his head as he disappeared among the men who were moving toward the stern and away from the advancing water.

"Where's Daddy? Where's Daddy?" Madge asked frantically.

"The women in one of the other boats said they wanted somebody to row for them, and Daddy got in that boat," said Lottie, lying for her child's sake but hoping it would be true.

When Lifeboat 14 neared capacity and no more women or children were in sight, Fifth Officer Harold Lowe jumped in and ordered it lowered. The crewmen on deck began carrying out his orders when Madge spotted a slender teenage schoolboy who was gripping the ship's rail and staring at Lowe. Although he didn't utter a word, she could tell from his wide, sad eyes that he was silently pleading for Lowe's permission to get in the craft. The officer saw him but ignored him.

Seconds before the lifeboat began its descent, the boy climbed onto the railing and, with a cry, leaped into the craft and scrambled under a seat in front of Lottie and Madge. Hoping to give the young man a chance, Lottie and another woman covered him up with their skirts.

Lowe pushed his way toward Lottie. Then he reached down, dragged the frightened lad out from under the seat, and ordered, "Get back on the ship!"

"Please, sir," the young man pleaded. "Let me stay. I won't take up much room."

Like most everyone in the lifeboat, Madge screamed when Lowe pulled out a revolver and pointed it at the head of the quivering lad. "I give you just ten seconds to get back onto that ship before I blow your brains out," Lowe hissed.

"Please, please," he begged. "I don't want to die."

Madge felt sorry for the young man and began to cry as did many of the women. Fearing that Lowe would carry out his threat, she gripped the officer's unarmed hand and pleaded, "Oh, Mr. Man, please don't shoot! Please don't shoot him!"

Lowe lowered his weapon and dropped his threatening tone. Looking at the boy squarely in the eyes, the officer told him, "For God's sake, be a man." Pointing to two stewards and a seaman who were handling the oars and tiller, Lowe added, "Other than me and three crewmen who'll man the boat, we've got only women and children on board."

Without saying a word, the tearful lad reluctantly climbed back over the railing and onto the deck of the *Titanic*. As the lifeboat was lowered, Madge caught a last glimpse of him. He was lying facedown near a coil of rope.

Just then several panic-stricken men charged the lifeboat. Lowe pulled out his weapon again and shouted, "If anyone else tries to get in, this is what he'll get!" Lowe fired his weapon three times in the air. Each shot caused Madge to cringe in her seat.

Once the lifeboat splashed into the water, the crewmen rowed furiously away from the *Titanic*. When No. 14 was a safe distance, Madge looked up in the crystal-clear moonless night. "Mummy, I didn't know there were that many stars in the sky," she said. For a few brief minutes, the dazzling twinkles above made her forget about the terror, confusion, and danger that shrouded the *Titanic*.

Lifeboat 14 was crammed tightly with 60 women and children. Lottie sat so close to one of the rowers that her ponytail occasionally got snagged in his oarlock, causing small chunks of her hair to be yanked out of her scalp. Madge could hear the band playing on the sinking ship. The musicians had changed from playing upbeat ragtime music to playing hymns, including one of her favorites, "Nearer My God to Thee." She thought she heard passengers on the ship weeping. "Those poor people are crying," Madge said.

"No, they're singing," replied Lowe, hoping his lie would minimize the anguish of the women and children in his lifeboat.

"They're no doubt praying, too," added Lottie.

Eventually, the music died, and the great *Titanic* slowly sank from sight. Then came the cries for help from those people who had jumped or been swept off the *Titanic* and were now flailing away in the deadly cold water. *One of them*, thought Madge, *could be Daddy*.

"We must go back and help them!" Lottie hollered.

But others in the lifeboat disagreed: "There's no more room." "They'll capsize our boat." "We can't help the poor souls. We need to save ourselves."

Lowe ignored the naysayers. "I'm in command of this boat, and what I say goes," he declared. "We will go back and help as many as possible."

"But we have no place to put them," claimed a passenger.

"We'll make room," said Lowe. He then rounded up Lifeboats 4, 10, 12, and D and had them tied together like a string of beads. To free up space in his boat, he moved several women and children into other boats that were less crowded. With the help of a few volunteers to man the oars, Lifeboat 14 headed back in an effort to look for any survivors.

It had been almost an hour since the *Titanic* sank, so the likelihood that anyone would still be alive in the frigid sea was slim at best. But No. 14 managed to pluck from the water a few barely conscious men—first-class steward John "Jack" Stewart, second-class passenger Charles Williams, and first-class passenger William Hoyt. But Hoyt was too far gone. He died within minutes of being pulled into the boat.

Madge and the others then spotted an Asian man who cleverly had used ropes to lash himself to a floating door. Lowe, like many Englishmen at the time, was prejudiced against Asians and didn't want to save him. "There are others better worth saving than the likes of him," said Lowe.

Madge couldn't believe her ears. She had been taught that all life was sacred.

Lottie spoke up. "Have you no common decency, Mr.

Lowe?" she protested. "We shall not leave this man to die when we have the means to save him."

Lowe sighed and said, "You're right."

The exhausted, shivering survivor was hauled into the lifeboat. Lottie and several other women took turns rubbing the man's feet, legs, arms, and chest to get his circulation going again. He soon perked up and then insisted on taking the place of a seaman who was too fatigued to row anymore. The Asian man rowed hard longer than anyone thought he could, prompting Lowe to admit, "I'd save the likes of him six times over if I got the chance."

Lifeboat 14 found no other survivors.

As the bone-numbing night wore on, Madge and Lottie remained huddled together and prayed that Harvey had been lucky enough to get into another lifeboat. The harsh cold triggered several coughing jags for Lottie. Madge shuddered uncontrollably until, overcome by exhaustion, she felt asleep in an upright position. Her mother did the same, but at one point she toppled forward, hitting her head on the seat in front of her.

Shortly before daybreak, the rescue ship *Carpathia* arrived on the scene and began picking up the survivors in the lifeboats. It was after 7 A.M. when the passengers from Lifeboat 14 were brought on board.

Given hot chocolate and a blanket, Madge kept waiting for her father to appear at any moment. But he wasn't in any of the lifeboats.

Still, Madge refused to give up hope, even after the *Carpathia* returned to New York. "Maybe Daddy got picked up by another ship," she told her mother.

After the *Carpathia* docked, the survivors were engulfed by reporters. Madge was interviewed by a reporter from the *Brooklyn Daily Eagle*, which published her story the next day. She described her harrowing escape from the sinking ship. "I was frightened a whole lot, and sometimes I cried," she told the reporter. "I cried hardest when I thought of my Dolly back there in the water with nobody to mind her and keep her from getting wet."

Within hours after New Yorkers read about Madge, they showered her with toys, clothes, and a doll. The new doll provided some comfort for Madge. But what she really wanted was to see her father again, to snuggle in his lap, to have him create a flower out of folded paper. Each day came and went without word of Harvey's fate. It seemed everyone but Madge had accepted that he had died at sea.

She and her mother had lost not only a father and husband but all their money. Their dream of a new life was shattered by sorrow and death—and now they were flat broke. Adding to their woes, Lottie needed medical attention for her lung problems. But with frcc medical care, assistance from the American Red Cross and the White Star Line, and donations from New Yorkers, mother and daughter had their immediate needs met.

Lottie's lungs improved quickly, but her heart remained broken. She blamed herself for Harvey's death, believing that if she had not suffered from lung ailments, they never would have considered moving to Idaho and, thus, would not have been on the *Titanic*. Despite her grief, she tried to remain strong for Madge's sake. Ironically, Lottie drew some of her strength from Madge—or at least Madge's refusal to accept that her father had perished.

On April 21, a week after the sinking, Lottie poured out her sorrow in this letter that she wrote to Harvey's parents (punctuation added):

My dear Mother and all,

I don't know how to write to you or what to say. I feel I shall go mad sometimes. But, dear, as much as my heart aches, it aches for you, too, for he is your son and the best that ever lived. I had not given up hope until today that he might be found, but I'm told all boats are accounted for. Oh, Mother, how can I live without him? I wish I'd gone with him. If they had not wrenched Madge from me, I would have stayed and gone with him. But they threw her into the boat and pulled me in, too. But he was so calm and I know he would rather I lived for her little sake, otherwise she would have been an orphan. The agony of that night can never be told. Poor mite was frozen. I have been ill but have been taken care of by a rich New York doctor and feel better now. . . .

Sometimes I feel we lived too much for each other. That is why I lost him. But, Mother, we shall meet him in heaven. When that band played "Nearer My God to Thee," I know he thought of you and me, for we both loved that hymn.

I feel that is why I [must] go to Payette. I'm doing what he would wish me to, so I hope to do this at the end of next week where I have friends and work. I will work for his darling [Madge] as long as she needs me. Oh, she is a comfort, but she doesn't realize yet that her Daddy is in heaven.

There are some dear children here who have loaded her with lovely toys, but it's when I'm alone with her that she misses him. Oh, Mother, I haven't a thing in the world that was his. Only his rings. Everything we had went down. . . .

God bless you, dear Mother, and help and comfort you in this awful sorrow.

Your loving child, Lot

In another letter to her in-laws the following week, Lottie expressed her anguish over Harvey's death and fears of an uncertain future. "Then I look at Madge [and] I feel braver. She is such a comfort," she wrote.

And yet nearly two weeks after the sinking, little Madge still believed that her daddy would miraculously appear. Lottie tried to explain the truth, but the young girl refused to listen. "I can't make Madge realize about Daddy," Lottie wrote, "so I must leave it to God and time to dull the awful shock it will be to her. . . ."

Harvey Collyer's body was never recovered. A memorial to him was erected at St. Mary's Church in Bishopstoke. Its inscription reads: "Sacred to the memory of Harvey Collyer, who fell asleep April 15, 1912. Age 31 years. Jesus said, 'Come.'"

In an attempt to carry out his dream, Lottie and Madge went to Payette, but it didn't work out for them. With the help of donations from friends, they soon returned to their home in Bishopstoke. Lottie remarried but died two years and three days after the sinking of the Titanic. Unwanted by her stepfather, Madge moved in with her father's brother Walter on a farm in East Horsley.

In 1927, when she was 23, Madge married Roy Dutton, the chief mechanic for a fleet of delivery vans. She never had children, so she filled her time gardening and caring for her dogs and cats. Madge died in 1965 at age 61.

Twenty years later, an undersea camera that took the first pictures of the debris field of the Titanic wreckage captured an image of a ceramic doll's head lying on the ocean floor.

"The Baby! Where's the Baby?"

John Collins

The bow of the *Titanic* was already submerged as icy water on the steeply sloping deck swirled around the knees of 17-year-old John Collins. Carrying a wailing baby boy in his arms, he started sloshing toward the stern.

It didn't matter that there weren't any lifeboats remaining back there, or that the ship was plunging to its death, or that he was just prolonging the inevitable. He had to do something, anything. After all, he was responsible for trying to save two lives.

He had taken only a few steps aft when an unexpected wave slammed into him, knocking him off his feet. Gasping for breath, John clutched the baby as the powerful force swept them off the deck and into the brutally cold ocean.

Never in his worst nightmare had he expected

anything so overwhelming as this—fighting for his life and that of an infant's as they were pulled under the surface.

Just a few hours earlier, John was relaxing and joking with some of the crewmen. At 9 P.M., he had finished his shift as an assistant cook in the first-class galley—a job he had signed up for only a week before the *Titanic*'s maiden voyage. The Irish-born lad had previously worked in the kitchen of the Ulster Reform Club, a meeting place for men of power in business and politics in John's hometown of Belfast.

Off duty on Sunday night, John walked up and down the corridor outside the crew's quarters and chatted with some of his fellow workers. He eventually plopped on his bunk and fell asleep about 10 P.M. Shortly after midnight, he was jolted awake by a commotion outside and by the roar of the steam valves on the ship's funnels. He threw on his pants, rushed into the hallway, and stopped one of the stewards.

"What's the matter?" John asked him.

"It seems we've struck an iceberg, mate."

John hurried outside and from his vantage point looked down into the well deck and was startled to see chunks of ice on the starboard side. But no one seemed too alarmed. In fact, several third-class passengers were having fun tossing ice at each other.

Stewards then passed word down the alleyway

that the ship was in no danger and that crewmembers should return to their bunks. But John wasn't convinced. When he went to bed, he stayed dressed. Soon he heard the thumping of many footsteps again, so he stepped out into the passageway and saw stewards in their white jackets hustling passengers toward the upper decks.

"I thought there was no problem," John said to a crewman.

"Well, there is now. Everyone is to get his life vest on and go to the Boat Deck at once. We're abandoning ship."

"Where should I go?"

"Try Lifeboat 16. Portside aft."

John raced toward the stern. When he reached No. 16 at about 1:30 A.M., he saw stokers, seamen, and passengers piling into the boat amid confusion and chaos. *I have no chance of getting in that one,* he thought. By this time, all but one of the standard-size lifeboats from amidships aft had been launched.

John was pivoting left and right trying to figure out his next move when a friend who was a steward grabbed his arm and said, "The last boats are toward the bow."

John hesitated. "But the bow is already underwater."

"Enjoy the swim then, mate." The steward took off.

John decided to join him and broke into a sprint,

weaving his way through people who were rushing up from steerage. When he caught up with his comrade, they encountered a woman in her twenties carrying a baby boy in one arm and holding the hand of a frightened little girl who looked about three years old. All three were crying. The woman seemed so flustered that she could hardly move and kept bawling, "Where do I go? I must save my son and daughter! Where do I go?"

John and the steward took pity on her. "Let us help you," said John. He took the baby from the woman while the steward picked up the girl. "Come with us," John told her. They ran to the port side on the Boat Deck, but they were too late. The last lifeboat from that section had just been launched. The ship was sinking at a faster rate now, pitching the deck at an alarmingly steep angle. Water was lapping up against the bridge.

From atop the officers' quarters at the base of the first funnel, a crewman shouted down to John and others, "A collapsible boat is getting launched from the starboard side! All women and children must hurry over there immediately!"

The ship had four special lifeboats, known as Englehardt collapsibles A, B, C, and D that could hold about 45 people each. Unlike the ship's 16 other lifeboats that were made of wood, these four had collapsible canvas sides so the boats could be stowed flat. Before these boats could be launched, their sides had to be pulled up and secured.

Cradling the baby in one arm, John grasped the woman's hand. Along with the steward who was carrying the girl, they dashed to the other side of the ship. Lifeboat A had already been taken off the roof of the officers' quarters, where it had been stowed. Crewmen were feverishly attaching it to the falls under the davits that had been used for Lifeboats 1 and C.

But time had all but run out. As the bow of the *Titanic* dipped deeper under the surface, water rushed over the deck, threatening to swamp Lifeboat A before they could release it. First class steward Edward Brown and another man leaped into the boat and cut the falls. Twenty people jumped in as a wave generated by the sinking ship washed it off the deck before anyone had a chance to put up the canvas sides.

Once again, John and his desperate little group were just a few seconds too late. "Oh, no!" the woman wailed. "What will we do now?"

John heard shouts of "Go aft! Go aft!" But he didn't need any urging. The only section of the ship that wasn't underwater was toward the stern. And that's where those left behind were fleeing.

"Follow me!" he yelled to his friend and the woman as the water rose to their knees. They wheeled around and started heading for the stern when a bone-chilling wave slammed into them, washing them right off the deck and into the icy water.

John let go of the woman's hand and threw his arms around the baby boy, squeezing him tightly to his chest to protect him. But a powerful force from the suction of the sinking ship dragged him under. Despite wearing his life vest, John found himself tumbling deeper below the surface.

Kicking furiously, he finally righted himself and headed toward the surface. But before he reached it, he became entangled in ropes and debris. His lungs crying out for air, John twisted and turned in a life-and-death struggle that seemed to last beyond what he thought possible. Suddenly, he broke free and spurted to the surface, gulping for air. *I'm still alive!*

Relief lasted for only a moment. *The baby! Where's the baby?* He spun around in a complete circle but couldn't see the infant anywhere. Somehow during John's fight for survival, the baby had been wrenched from his grasp. Ignoring the freezing cold that was sapping his strength, John shoved aside floating deck chairs, tables, and other debris in a frantic search for the little guy.

But then, from seemingly nowhere, a man leaped on John's back and shoved him under. John felt the man's strong arms wrap around his neck in a deadly choke hold. John was nearly out of breath when he finally pried apart the death grip and squirmed free. Wheezing, John screamed, "Get away from me!"

The man, who wasn't wearing a life jacket, was thrashing wildly a few feet away. Coughing and spitting up water, he pleaded, "Help me! I'm drowning!" He lunged for John again. This time John was ready and propelled himself out of the panic-stricken man's reach. John grabbed a floating deck chair, shoved it over to him, and said, "Use this. I can't save you. I'll be lucky if I can save myself." As John swam away, he told himself, *He's going to drown. But if I tried to help him, in the state of mind he's in, we'd both end up dead.*

John no longer thought about the lost infant. He couldn't. His mind was focused on one thing and one thing only—survival. And that meant getting out of the water before the cold killed him.

In the darkness, he spotted something a few yards away that looked like a giant clam. Swimming closer, John discovered it was an overturned lifeboat. It was Lifeboat B (the same one that 17-year-old John Thayer clung to) with about 15 or 20 shivering men sitting or sprawled on its exposed hull. After reaching the upside-down craft, he lurched out of the water with a mighty kick and climbed to safety, draping himself over the keel. No one said a word. He understood why. They were just as exhausted and miserable as he was.

Then he watched in utter disbelief as the *Titanic*

split in two and disappeared below the surface, leaving hundreds of victims flailing about in the water, begging for help.

A few more crewmen and passengers managed to reach the overturned craft and climbed aboard. Looking like a big, waterlogged shaggy dog, a man wearing a fur coat over his life jacket climbed on. He was Colonel Archibald Gracie, a retired military officer who would later be praised for his tireless efforts in assisting women and children into lifeboats. After being swept off the deck, Gracie had floated on a large wooden crate before he made it onto the hull.

After each new person got on, the overturned boat sank a little lower and became less steady, causing grave concern. A crewman who had the craft's only oar began swatting at anyone who came near.

"Dear God, man, save one life!" begged a swimmer, who was beaten back. Not giving up, the swimmer paddled to the other side of the hull and got on.

When an older man in a life vest approached Lifeboat B, the men began yelling at him not to climb on because they were afraid he'd tip it over and spill them in the water.

"That's all right, boys," he replied through chattering teeth. "Keep cool and God bless you. Good-bye."

Watching him swim away, John couldn't help but wonder if they had just sent the man to his death.

Another swimmer saw that there was no room on the hull and didn't even ask for help. Instead, he croaked, "Good lads!" John saw him take a deep breath, then fall silent and motionless as he drifted out of sight.

Commenting on the swimmers who didn't get on, Gracie told the group, "There go men of grace and dignity in the face of death. I saw a lot of that gallantry tonight—even among the women. Mrs. Ida Straus for one. Her husband, Isidor—the man who owns Macy's department store—declined the chance to board a lifeboat. Many of us tried to convince Mrs. Straus to get into one but she absolutely refused. She told us, 'I've always stayed with my husband, so why should I leave him now?' When I last saw them, they were sitting on deck chairs, holding hands."

Sagging under the weight of more than two dozen shuddering, weakening men, Lifeboat B floated in the quiet darkness. One of the crewmembers asked the group, "Don't you think we ought to pray?" They settled on reciting the Lord's Prayer. They also elected Charles Lightoller, the *Titanic*'s second officer, as their "commander" and agreed to follow his orders.

Their overturned boat kept sinking ever so slowly as the night grew colder, making life aboard the exposed hull even bleaker. John's thick dark hair had frozen, his muscles ached, and he couldn't stop shivering. It was the same for most everyone. To pass the time, some talked about their final minutes aboard the *Titanic*.

Lightoller said he dived in the water from atop the officer's quarters and tried to swim clear of the ship. But he was sucked back and pinned against the grate of the first funnel's ventilator shaft by seawater rushing into it. Expecting to die because he couldn't free himself, Lightoller was miraculously saved when a boiler exploded. The force of the blast coming up from the shaft blew him to the surface, and he paddled clear.

Chief baker Charles Joughin said he began tossing deck chairs overboard for people to use as little rafts. Then he worked his way to the rising stern. At the very back, he climbed over the railing so that he was standing outside of it. He held on to the railing as the back section of the ship began its plunge. Riding the stern all the way down to the waterline like an elevator, Joughin stepped off into the sea.

Harold Bride, 22, the assistant wireless operator, said he had been trying to help a group of men lower Lifeboat B when they were washed off the ship by the same wave that swept John and others into the sea. The wave had flipped the boat over hull-side-up, trapping Bride underneath. But he managed to wriggle out from under it and get on.

When Lightoller learned that Bride was aboard, he asked, "Did you contact any ships?"

"Yes, the *Carpathia*, *Baltic*, and *Olympic*. The

Carpathia is the closest. She is coming up as fast as she can from the southeast. She knows our position. There is no mistake. We should see her lights before daybreak."

Hearing that report bolstered John's spirits. But as the night dragged on, he wondered if he could survive the unbearable cold and if the upside-down hull could stay afloat until the rescue ship arrived. Toward dawn, it turned colder and breezier. Waves splashed over him and the others, the saltwater stinging his eyes. The parts of his body that weren't completely numb were throbbing in pain, causing him to wonder how much misery a human could endure. Some couldn't bear the suffering anymore. Throughout the night, several slid or rolled off and disappeared without a sound.

Jack Phillips, the chief wireless operator, took his last breath on the overturned craft. "He was a brave man," said Bride. "He stuck to his work while everybody else was raging about. Captain Smith had released him from duty. But Phillips kept sending messages to the *Carpathia* right up until the last moment."

When the waves kicked up, Lightoller had the weary, frozen men stand up and shift their weight in unison to keep their rocking, sinking boat afloat. Dog tired, John kept scanning the southeast horizon, waiting for the first sign that the rescue ship had arrived. He didn't know how much longer he could hold out.

"There, to the southeast! There it is!" came a shout. John looked up and saw a glorious sight—a green flare far off in the distance. "It's the *Carpathia* telling us that help is on the way!"

The men cheered. But their happiness soon was tempered when they saw that the ship had stopped about four miles away. While the vessel began picking up survivors from other lifeboats shortly after 4 A.M., Lifeboat B was barely floating.

Although he was soaked to the bone, John did not want to end up back in the frigid water. In his weakened state, it would probably mean death. But soon the light of dawn revealed a string of lifeboats only a half mile away. Lightoller hailed them over with a whistle and then organized a transfer. John and about half the men hopped into No. 12 while the rest climbed into No. 4. They also brought with them the body of Jack Phillips.

Eventually, all the survivors were brought aboard the *Carpathia*. John vowed then and there that when he got back home to Ireland, he would never sail again.

John Collins remained in New York for two weeks so he could testify before a special panel of the U.S. Senate Commerce Committee investigating the Titanic *tragedy. At 17 years old, John was the youngest person to testify at the hearings.*

Not much is known about him after he returned

to his home in Belfast, Northern Ireland. He served in World War I and became a prisoner of war in Germany. During his imprisonment, John entertained other prisoners with his stories of survival on the Titanic. He died in Belfast in 1941 at age 45.

The identity of the baby John tried to save can't be confirmed. However, many historians believe he was seven-month-old Alfred Peacock, son of Mrs. Edith Peacock, 26, of Southampton, England, and brother of Treasteall Peacock, a three-year-old girl. In 1911, Edith and her husband, Benjamin, a mechanical engineer, had decided to immigrate to Elizabeth, New Jersey. But shortly before the family was to sail, Edith fell ill so her husband went to America alone. Edith and the children planned to join him once she was strong enough to travel.

The bodies of Edith, Treasteall, and Alfred were never recovered.

Glossary

A Deck—on the *Titanic,* the first deck below the top deck (Boat Deck) followed by Decks B through G, plus two additional decks below them

aft—toward the ship's rear

amidships—toward the ship's middle

bailer—a handheld container used for removing water from a boat

berth—single bed in a shared room

Boat Deck—the top deck on the *Titanic* that held the lifeboats

boatswain's chair—a wooden seat between two ropes, much like a swing, and used to hoist or lower a person over the ship's side

boiler—on the *Titanic,* a steel container in which water was boiled to create the steam that turned the turbine

bollard—metal post on a ship or dock around which mooring lines are tied

bow—the front end of the ship

bridge—a raised structure toward the front of the ship, which has an unobstructed view ahead and houses the navigating instruments, the wheel, and other devices needed to operate the ship

bulkhead—a dividing wall in the hull that separates compartments on a ship

cabin—a room on a ship

collapsible lifeboat—a lifeboat with pull-up canvas sides

companionway—a staircase leading from a deck to the cabins or areas below

crow's nest—a lookout platform high on a ship's mast

davits—cranelike arms used for holding up and lowering lifeboats

falls—ropes used to lower a lifeboat from the davits

fore—at or near the bow

funnel—a ship's smokestack

gangway—a ramp from the dock to an opening in the side of a ship

grog—a drink made of rum, water, sugar, and lemon

growler—a small, flat iceberg that has broken off from a larger one

hawser—a large rope used for towing or mooring

hold—a storage space for cargo belowdecks

hot toddy—a mixture of brandy or rum with sugar, hot water, and spices

hull—lower frame of a ship

ice field—a large level expanse of floating ice more than five miles wide

Jacob's ladder—a ladder that hooks on the side of the ship and has rope sides with wood rungs on which to climb

keel—the center line running fore and aft along the bottom of a ship

knot—a unit of speed equal to one nautical mile (6,080 feet) per hour

lifting—tilting of a ship to one side

maiden voyage—first trip by a ship

Marconi—the wireless radio invented by Guglielmo Marconi

passageway—a corridor on a ship

port—the left side when looking at the bow from the stern

promenade—an upper deck on which passengers can stroll

purser—the person on a ship responsible for the handling of money on board and for attending to the passengers' welfare

quartermaster—the person on a ship who supervises deck staff on maintenance, cleaning, and daily duties as well as the loading and unloading of supplies and luggage

quarters—living spaces for passengers or personnel; also, individual stations for personnel for fire or boat drills

quoits—a ring-toss game

RMS—Royal Mail Ship

rocket—a fireworkslike flare used as a distress signal

starboard—the right side when looking at the bow from the stern

stateroom—a more luxurious private room or cabin for passengers or officers

steerage—the cheapest and least desirable accommodations for passengers in the lowest decks

stern—the rear end of the ship

steward—a crewmember who attends to the needs of passengers

stoker—a crewmember who tends the ship's boilers

tender—a small boat that takes passengers and luggage from the dock to a ship anchored in the harbor

watch—division of time, usually four hours each, for standing watch or being on deck ready for duty

wireless—an early form of long distance radio

About the Author

Allan Zullo is the author of more than 100 nonfiction books on subjects ranging from sports and the supernatural to history and animals.

He has introduced Scholastic readers to the Ten True Tales series, gripping stories of extraordinary persons—many of them young people—who have met the challenges of dangerous, sometimes life-threatening, situations. Among the books in the series are *Heroes of 9/11, War Heroes: Voices from Iraq,* and *Battle Heroes: Voices from Afghanistan.* In addition, he has authored three books about the real-life experiences of kids during the Holocaust—*Survivors: True Stories of Children in the Holocaust, Heroes of the Holocaust: True Stories of Rescues by Teens,* and *Escape: Children of the Holocaust.*

Allan, the grandfather of five and the father of two grown daughters, lives with his wife, Kathryn, on the side of a mountain near Asheville, North Carolina. To learn more about the author, visit his website at www.allanzullo.com.